Curtis

1907–47

KEY
Books

AVIATION INDUSTRY SERIES, VOLUME 6

Front cover image: Hangar 11 owner, Peter Teichman, at the controls of the collection's P-40M in the markings of the 343rd Fighter Group. Built in October 1943, the fighter is the only airworthy example of the P-40M outside of the USA and New Zealand. (Darren Harbar Photography (www.darrenharbar.co.uk))

Title page image: Ordered by the US Navy as the F8C-3, all 21 aircraft were delivered as the observation OC-2. The type served until October 1935, when the last machine with 2,511 flying hours to its credit was scrapped.

Contents page image: A display of force by the United States Army Air Corps (USAAC) as 18 Curtiss A-12 Shrikes show off to the cameras during an exercise in the mid-1930s.

Back cover image: Curtiss SBC-4 Helldiver 1318 of the Seattle reserve on approach into Oakland in July 1940. (Bill Larkins)

Published by Key Books
An imprint of Key Publishing Ltd
PO Box 100
Stamford
Lincs PE9 1XQ

www.keypublishing.com

Original edition published as *Aeroplane's Curtiss Company Profile 1907–1947* © 2014, edited by Martyn Chorlton

This edition © 2023

ISBN 978 1 80282 373 8

All images are from Martyn Chorlton's collection unless otherwise specified.

Typeset by SJmagic DESIGN SERVICES, India.

Contents

Introduction

Curtiss, the company, was a significant contributor in establishing the US aircraft industry on the world stage. Behind this great company was one forward-thinking Glenn Hammond Curtiss. He was a multi-talented engineer and a good businessman. It was this latter ability that would see the Curtiss Aeroplane and Motor Company grow into a huge organization within a short period of time. By the end of World War One, Curtiss had built more than 10,000 aircraft and, unlike other similar companies, did not capsize once the conflict was over, and the military contracts were cancelled.

Glenn Curtiss began to distance himself from his own company from the early 1920s but would remain a director until his premature death in 1930. The company merged to become Curtiss-Wright in 1929, and it's possible it may have followed a different path if Glenn Curtiss had continued his original proactive role at the helm. Ultimately, the lack of research and development invested in the company leading up to the jet age saw the premature demise of Curtiss-Wright. Its aircraft manufactured in the lead up to World War Two were not the best, but the company's business-like approach to aircraft manufacturing meant that it could produce large volumes for a variety of customers, including those overseas, at a reasonable price.

The story of one of the company's most famous aircraft, Curtiss P-40 Warhawk, was a political one, which effectively allowed an inferior aircraft to stay in production for almost three years longer than it should have, bringing great wealth to Curtiss-Wright. This wealth was not reinvested in the company, however, and in 1947 its attempt to break into the arena of jet aircraft production failed, and the aviation side of Curtiss-Wright was sold to North American Aviation.

The Curtiss-Wright Corporation is a huge, profitable company to this day, still working with the aerospace industry and defence, as well as oil and gas and the nuclear power-generation industries.

Not every single Curtiss and Curtiss-Wright aircraft produced during the 40 years of the company's existence in the aircraft industry is included here, though many of the 120 types are mentioned.

An early production Curtiss P-40 in company with an SBC Helldiver (one of three Curtiss aircraft to use this name).

The Curtiss Story

A passion for speed

Born in Hammondsport, New York, on May 21, 1878, Glenn Hammond Curtiss was not highly educated, but from an early age he showed an aptitude for all things mechanical and all competitive sports. He was inventive too. In 1890, the family moved to Rochester, New York, and at 12 years old he began working, after school, as a telegraph messenger for Western Union. Curtiss's saw first-hand the transformative power of electricity and he was inventive enough to build his own basic communication system.

His first full-time job was with the Eastman Dry Plate and Film Company, later more familiarly known as the Eastman Kodak Company. Employed to assemble cameras, Curtiss learnt the skill set to build his own camera so that he could study how photography worked in more detail. He also invented a stencil machine, which was subsequently used by the company. This early association with Kodak made an impression on Curtiss and he would later fully employ the power of the photographic image to record every aspect of his later aviation work.

Glenn Hammond Curtiss at work, with one of his early amphibian pushers, prior to World War one. Virtually every aspect of his work was recorded on film.

Bicycle and motorcycle manufacturer

In 1897, Curtiss returned to his home town of Hammondsport where he found work in a bicycle repair shop. After just three years, he had established his first business, the GH Curtiss Manufacturing Company, specializing in bicycles.

Combining his natural business and engineering skills, Curtiss soon modified a bicycle to take a small petrol engine. This first motorcycle was fitted with his own single-cylinder engine, complete with a carburettor manufactured from a soup can! The Hammondsport factory began to expand as motorcycle manufacturing joined with bicycle-manufacturing, and at the same time the company became an agent for several different car companies.

The Curtiss motorcycles were competitive machines, and in 1903 Curtiss gained the motorcycle land speed record, achieving 64mph, over a one-mile long course at Yonkers, New York. Curtiss went on to win endurance races against companies and teams with much bigger

Louis Paulhan, a pioneering French aviator with Glenn Curtiss at the Los Angeles Air Meet in 1910.

Flying-boat pioneer, Lt (later Col) John Cyril Porte with Glenn Curtiss. Porte was instrumental in modifying the hull of the Curtiss H.12, which created the excellent Felixstowe F.2 and later F.3.

budgets and engineering support, and captured the ten-mile world speed record in 1904. That same year, Curtiss is credited with inventing the traditional handlebar throttle control, which remains the standard way of controlling the speed of a motorcycle to this day. Curtiss quickly gained a reputation for quality and reliability for his motorcycle designs and engine performance.

Speed remained one of his priorities and, on January 24, 1907, Curtiss established an unofficial world motorcycle land speed record of 136.36mph on a V8 machine at Ormond Beach, Florida. This record would stand until 1930 and would help to establish the company's reputation for high-performance engines.

Airship engines

Early balloonist Thomas Scott Baldwin was attracted to the Curtiss motorcycle engines because of their high power-to-weight ratio. Baldwin first established a balloon factory in San Francisco in 1904 and it was from there that the first controllable dirigible balloon in the US, named *California Arrow*, made its first flight on August 3, 1904. The engine for the *California Arrow* was made by Curtiss and following this success, a close business association between the two entrepreneurs formed. Baldwin moved his factory to Hammondsport in 1906 so that he could collaborate with Curtiss on various propulsion methods for airships. Experimental work incorporated propellers for airships using various tricycle "wind wagons" and even an iceboat.

Curtiss developed engines for airships very quickly and, by 1906, it was claimed that every airship flying in the US was powered by a Curtiss engine. Baldwin went on to design the Signal Corps Dirigible Number 1 (SC-1), which was powered by a 20hp Curtiss engine. This machine was destined to be the US Army's first "aircraft," which was purchased for the sum of $5,737.50 in August 1908.

The first of many "Jenny" JN Trainers pictured at Hammondsport prior to delivery to the US Army.

Aerial Experiment Association

Thanks to the success of the airship engines, Curtiss established his name in aeronautical circles across the US. At the same time, telephone inventor, Alexander Graham Bell, formed the Aerial Experiment Association (AEA). Bell was enthusiastic to get Curtiss on board, describing him as "the greatest motor expert in the country," with regard to heavier-than-air flight. Formed on October 1, 1907, the AEA was invested with the sole purpose of "…constructing a practical aerodrome, driven by its own motive power, and carrying a man". AEA notable members included Canadian JAD McCurdy, Lt Thomas Selfridge of the US Army, and FW "Casey" Baldwin (no relation to the dirigible pioneer), while Curtiss served as Director of Experiments. A period of research followed, and it was decided that each member of the association would design their own aerodrome*, to be funded and built by the AEA. However, no single aircraft would be credited to one man, as each design would receive input from all members. Bell had already been experimenting with tetrahedral kites and had reached a stage where he wanted to add an engine.

Curtiss is credited with contributing ingenuity and experience to the AEA rather than funds, which were solely provided by Bell's wife, Mabel, who gave $35,000 to the association. The resulting aerodromes produced by the AEA were an accumulation of aeronautical experience, which in turn, accrued valuable knowledge for the aviators. Both propeller and engine research were advanced in the US, with Curtiss using "wind wagons" to power his inventions. However, after the aerodromes had been produced, the Wright Brothers claimed that some details of their aircraft had been incorporated into the AEA designs. Both Curtiss and Baldwin had visited the Wright Brothers while they were in Dayton during an airshow, and Curtiss visited to sell them engines, but no details of their aircraft were ever sought or used, although there was discussion about propeller design.

In 1908, the first of four successful aerodromes was flown by the AEA, followed by Bell's tetrahedral kite, which lifted a man for the first time in 1909. These early aircraft, although not Curtiss designs, are often seen as the building blocks for his company's first foray into aircraft manufacturing, which began in 1909. His first aircraft, the Curtiss No.1 "Gold Bug" or "Golden Flyer," drew heavily on the knowledge gathered by the association, and was developed with the full approval of the AEA. By 1909, the planned research work was completed by the AEA, and with no plans to enter into production, the

A Liberty-powered F.2B Fighter converted by Curtiss, which ultimately proved unsuccessful because of the heavier American engine over the original Rolls-Royce Eagle.

---

* *a contemporary term for an airplane*

pre-arranged dissolution date for the association of 31 March was adhered to. Several AEA patents were applied for and, under the control of trustees, remained the property of all the original founders.

Pre-war accomplishments

Post AEA, Glenn Curtiss began designing and building aircraft, including two major production machines – the Curtiss pusher and single-engine pusher flying-boat. An example of the former was fitted with pontoons in 1911, and became the world's first successful seaplane.

Curtiss made his first sale to the New York Aeronautical Society and this was followed by the sale of individual aircraft to private order. However, Curtiss's main income, at the time, was from his own exhibition flying as well as that of a few select company pilots, including Eugene Ely, Charles Hamilton and Hugh Robinson. Because of the success of display flying, this venture was formed into the Curtiss Exhibition Company on July 30, 1910, and the new company ran several Curtiss flying schools.

Glenn Curtiss and his aircraft achieved a number of early successes, including the Scientific American Trophy in his Golden Flyer and winning the first International Gordon Bennett Race, in France, in August 1909. Curtiss won the Scientific American Trophy for a third time in May 1910, which meant he permanently held the trophy, after flying an 150-mile flight from Albany, New York, to Governor's Island, New York harbour. Curtiss won the Collier Trophy for his work in developing the hydro-airplane or seaplane in 1912 and 1913; the latter for his work with flying-boats.

Curtiss was well aware of the potential of aircraft for military purposes; but at that time, both the US Army and Navy were apathetic towards flying machines. The Army tentatively bought a single Baldwin airship in 1908 and a Wright biplane in 1909, while the Navy was disinterested until 1911. Curtiss was fortunate to know a number of senior naval officers who were more enterprizing in spirit than the institution for which they worked, and from late 1910, began a series of demonstrations to show the Navy how useful aircraft could be. Firstly, Eugene Ely successfully flew a 50hp Curtiss pusher off a wooden platform mounted on the forward deck of USS *Birmingham*, anchored in Hampton Roads, Virginia, on November 10, 1910. Ely impressed the Navy a second time on January 18, 1911, when he landed a pusher on the after deck of the USS *Pennsylvania* in San Francisco Bay. Glenn Curtiss followed this achievement by landing a seaplane alongside the *Pennsylvania*, which was then anchored in San Diego Bay, and was winched aboard, the exercise being reversed when he departed. Prior to this, Curtiss had also written to the Secretary of the Navy, in November 1910, offering to teach a naval officer to fly, for free. Once the Navy officer passed his flight training, the US Navy bought two Curtiss machines. The same shrewd method of generating interest in aviation also worked with the Army.

New York State was not the best place to learn to fly, since its winters are particularly harsh. Curtiss searched for more suitable locations with good weather all year around, settling for the barren, yet flat, North Island in San Diego Bay. After obtaining a three-year lease for the whole island, a flying school was established there in 1910 and operated from November 25 through to April 25. By November 1912, a section of the island had been sub-leased to the US Army for its own new flying school, and in 1917, the US Navy moved in as well. The island was shared by the US Army and US Navy until 1932 when the latter took over the site, which remains a prominent US Naval Air Station to this day.

Glenn Curtiss continued to create new companies. From 1909, he had been in a tenuous partnership with Augustus M Herring as the Herring-Curtiss Company. Now alongside the Curtiss Exhibition Company, he established the Curtiss Aeroplane Company on December 1, 1910, and the Curtiss Motor Company on December 19, 1911.

By late 1912, the Curtiss and Wright Companies had reached a point where they could not develop their pusher designs any further, and since an increasing number of other manufacturers were designing a more efficient tractor configuration, Curtiss moved in a similar direction. Lacking expertise in tractor design Curtiss employed a British engineer, ex-Sopwith employee B D Thomas, to produce new aircraft. Thomas began work on the successful Model J before he crossed the Atlantic and would later contribute to the Model N and "America" flying-boat.

The development of the seaplane was another of Glenn Curtiss's great passions, and he is widely recognized as the inventor of the "practical" seaplane. Float design and familiar stepped hulls started to appear from 1912. A single main float configuration combined with wingtip floats was used for the majority of US Navy seaplanes until the 1960s. While these early aircraft were basically landplanes, which were re-configured to operate from water, the flying-boat, with its boat-like integrated hull, was designed from the outset for the task. Glenn Curtiss is recognized as creating the flying-boat configuration beginning with Flying-boat No.1, which first appeared in January 1912. Unsuccessful, it was quickly superseded by Flying-boat No.2 "The Flying Fish," which featured a full-length, flat-bottomed hull.

World War One

When war broke out in Europe in August 1914, aircraft development in the US continued at sedentary speed, while Britain, France and Germany advanced their military machines at great pace. While the US remained neutral in the conflict, no European country would share its technology with America and, as a result, when the US joined the war in April 1917, not one combat aircraft was available. US manufacturers received a number of orders from Europe, but up to 1917, these tended to be for trainers, two-seat reconnaissance machines and cumbersome patrol flying-boats.

Curtiss was in the most advantageous position of all US aircraft manufacturers because the company was already supplying Europe, especially with large numbers of the F-boat. The "America" flying-boats were purchased by the Royal Navy and orders followed for more improved versions. The UK also placed large orders for the JN trainer and the Model R, and it was not long before the Hammondsport facility was unable to handle the number of orders. A new factory was sourced in the large industrial city of Buffalo, New York, close to Lake Erie. With an abundance of labour and power and a transport network, Buffalo was everything Hammondsport was not. However, the former site was retained for engine manufacturing.

At first, Curtiss leased an area of the Thomas Power Building, but following increased orders from Britain, this location proved to be inadequate and a new 110,000 sq/ft factory was built. Work began on March 10, 1915, and, by May 15, the new factory, called the Churchill plant, was rolling out its first aircraft. Not long after, the Century Telephone Building was taken over by Curtiss for engine production and renamed the South Elmwood plant. Further factories in Austin and Bradley Street were also turned over to aircraft manufacturing, but more and much bigger were yet to come. When the US joined World War One, the biggest aircraft factory in the world, covering 72 acres, was added to the South Elmwood plant and become known as the North Elmwood plant. The factory was built from July to October 1917, at a cost of $4 million.

The Curtiss organization reorganized following the move to Buffalo, which saw the creation of the Curtiss Aeroplane and Motor Company. Some flight testing was carried out at Buffalo and, during the summer, at the Curtiss flying school in Virginia. Development of new types during this period was purely speculative as the US Army had no aircraft combat experience and was not sure exactly what it would need in Europe. As a result, Curtiss established an experimental centre, under the control of the Curtiss Engineering Corporation, based at Hazelhurst Field, Garden City, Long Island. By late 1917, the big Curtiss plants were being managed by men from the motor industry, while the aviation engineers were tasked with introducing design ideas, which was where Glenn Curtiss was at home.

In late 1917, more than 18,000 people worked in the Buffalo plant, and Glenn Curtiss felt a personal responsibility to build as many aircraft as possible. In April 1917, when orders came flooding in from the US War Department, Curtiss was by far the largest aircraft manufacturer and one of 16 companies that could handle the workload; in comparison, at least six of the firms that were approached had only built ten or aircraft or less.

In 1918, the War Department established the Aircraft Production Board (APB) to control aircraft manufacturing across the country. One of the APB's tasks was to travel to Europe to choose several designs suitable for massed production in America. It was hoped that this would speed up the entry into service of more modern machines for the US Army. All US aircraft manufacturers were ordered not to develop any aircraft of their own for the remainder of the war. Curtiss's order book filled with JN trainers, N-9 trainers for the US Navy, and F- and H-series flying-boats. An order for 3,000 Spad XIIIs was placed by the APB in September 1917, only to be cancelled on November 7, followed by an order for 2,000 Bristol F.2b fighters. Originally powered by a 250hp Rolls-Royce Eagle, the F.2b was redesigned to take a Liberty engine but after only 26 were built, this order was also cancelled in July 1918. Five hundred Caproni bombers and 1,000 RAF SE.5s were also ordered, only to be cancelled later.

The APB soon gave up the idea of trying to adapt European designs to American manufacturing techniques, and by early 1918, it allowed the industry to continue to designing its own aircraft. It was all too late by then, however, as new aircraft did not start appearing until the summer of 1918, and by the time they were through their test programmes, the war had ended. Between July 1917 and March 1919, the US government had put aside $640 million for the aviation programme. Of this, Curtiss received $90 million, and during this period delivered 5,221 aircraft (33 percent of all US aircraft production) and 5,000 engines.

Post-war survival

The predicted rosy post-war period, which would see the fledgling air force and civilian markets ordering hundreds of new aircraft never came. Virtually all military contracts were cancelled soon after the Armistice, leaving small companies to flounder and forcing larger companies to shut down many facilities. Curtiss was forced to close all but nine of its factories; leaving only one in Buffalo and the Curtiss Engineering Corporation in Garden City. All of the 'car-minded' senior management moved on, leaving Curtiss to return to running the business as it had been before the war.

Curtiss had several military projects to complete after the war and was optimistic enough about the civilian market to revive the Curtiss Exhibition Company, open several new flying schools, expand its network of dealerships, and set up the new Curtiss Export Company, in anticipation of foreign sales. Curtiss even purchased the US Army aerodrome at Hazelhurst Field and renamed it Curtiss Field. It was all to no avail and work on civilian models came to an abrupt end in June 1920.

The United States Army Air Service (USAAS) made do with what it owned once the war ended. The market was awash with ex-military aircraft at this time, but Curtiss overcame this when it bought a batch of airframes, engines and equipment direct from the US government for just $2.7 million. These aircraft cost the taxpayer $20 million, and at the time, great controversy surrounded the deal, mainly because it was carried out before the items were made available for the public to buy. However, the bulk of the aircraft were in no fit state to be flown by civilian pilots and the cost of refurbishment was something that the government was not prepared to pay for. Equally large in number were Curtiss's own aircraft, which were still in the packing cases.

Curtiss maintained its position during the 1920s as the lead US aircraft manufacturer thanks to its excellent facilities and experienced staff. All new aircraft work through to 1925 was with military aircraft, and during this period, the company made several innovative contributions to the industry. These included the D-12 engine, the PW-8, which was the first post-war-designed pursuit aircraft to go into production, and the record-breaking military racers. General aircraft design did not evolve a great deal other than a gradual departure from wooden fuselage construction to welded steel or bolted aluminium frames. It was not until 1926 that the civilian market began to germinate again as the many military surplus types came to end of their natural lives.

Curtiss-Wright and World War Two

On July 5, 1929, the Curtiss Aeroplane and Motor Company merged with the Wright Aeronautical Corporation (ex-Wright Company) to form the huge Curtiss-Wright Corporation. Twelve companies in total formed the merger, which had its headquarters in Buffalo, and had $75 million to its credit, making it by far the largest aviation company in the US.

Divided into three main divisions, the new company comprised the Curtiss-Wright Airplane Division, which was responsible for the manufacture of airframes; the Wright Aeronautical Corporation, which made engines; and the Curtiss-Wright Propeller Division. As big as it was, Curtiss-Wright struggled to survive the Great Depression through the early 1930s; during this time, it was the engine division that kept the company going thanks to its close and long relationship with the military.

By the late 1930s, the entire aircraft industry was booming, and military machines, in particular, were in great demand. The arrival of the P-36 was timely for Curtiss-Wright; the company produced the largest peace-time order for a military aircraft ever committed to by the USAAC. Also known as the Hawk, the little fighter sold well abroad, especially to the French and later to the British who were preparing for another war in Europe.

When World War Two began, aircraft production ramped up; the P-40 broke all records with almost 14,000 produced. More than 7,000 SB2C Helldivers were built for the US Navy and more than 3,000 C-46s helped to keep the US Army, Navy and United States Marine Corps (USMC) moving in every theatre of the war. The P-40 family was by far the company's greatest achievement; the little fighter remained in production from 1940 through to 1944. Despite its many failings, when used correctly, the aircraft was an effective fighting machine and this was proven early on during its service with Claire Chennault's 1st American Volunteer Group (AVG) aka "The Flying Tigers," which fought the Japanese straight after Pearl Harbor. Production of the P-40 was ostensibly carried out in Buffalo, Columbus, St Louis and Louisville, while the engine and propellers were churned out at factories in New Jersey, Pennsylvania and Ohio.

The busy flight deck of USS *Lexington* (CV-2) in 1928, with Curtiss F6C-3s of VF-5 on board.

Some of the 13,738 P-40s built by Curtiss between 1939 and 1944 at an average cost of $44,892 (1944) each.

Another successful product in demand by the US Navy for much of the war was the SBC-2 Helldiver. With the exception of the C-46, the Helldiver was the only other Curtiss product to see extensive post-war service.

The Louisville factory in Kentucky was allocated, in May 1942, for the production of a transport aircraft to be built from non-priority materials. The effectively meant using wood as it was feared that stocks of aluminium would run out at the rate at which aircraft were built. By this stage of the war, Curtiss-Wright had come up with the C-76 Caravan, which had some novel features, not to mention its wooden construction. Only a few rolled off the Louisville production line before the US government realized that the aluminium supply was not destined to run dry and so the C-76 was cancelled. As a consolation prize, the Louisville plant began production of the C-46 Commando, eventually contributing more than 400 to the final total; the rest were all built at Buffalo. The C-46 was a success story in its own right, the cargo aircraft was able to carry much heavier loads at a greater height than its C-47 counterpart.

By the end of World War Two, Curtiss-Wright could boast some very impressive production figures. These include 29,269 aircraft built, 142,840 engines and 146,468 electric propellers manufactured, and at its peak, a workforce of 180,000 people. It only trailed General Motors with regard to the total value of its World War Two contracts.

Post World War Two

Curtiss-Wright had ridden the wave of colossal orders during World War Two with vigour and serious success but when the contracts were slashed at the end of the conflict, the company had very little to fall back on. It had been very lucky with the P-40, a marginal development on the pre-war P-36 but the company's inclination to research and develop the next model in small steps would be its undoing. Curtiss-Wright had invested in its infrastructure but not in developing and researching new aircraft, especially when the jet-age arrived in 1943. Other aircraft manufacturers such as Bell, Lockheed, North American, and Northrop had all invested in the research and development of new wings, airframes and engines, which included jets. As a result Curtiss-Wright missed out on post-war orders. Only the XF-87 Blackhawk reached the prototype stage, and was beaten into production by the F-89 Scorpion. When the Blackhawk was cancelled on October 10, 1948, the entire Aeroplane Division was sold off by Curtiss-Wright to North American.

The legacy of Glenn H Curtiss

Following the re-organization of Curtiss in 1920, Glenn Curtiss took a step back from the company that he had created, and moved to Florida with his family. He would remain a director but total control of Curtiss was now in the hands of Clement M Keys. After having cashed in his stock, Glenn Curtiss was one of the richest men in the US, with approximately $32 million to his name. He immersed himself in the Florida lifestyle and, along with James Bright, co-developed the city of Hialeah in 1921 and later Miami Springs in 1923. In the former, he also established the Hialeah Park Race Track, and at the latter, he built an airport, which operated a flying school. He also contributed a great deal to the development of Opa-Locka where an airport was also established. He donated large areas of land and water rights during his time in Florida, which was cut short on July 23, 1930, when he passed away in Buffalo after contesting one of the many lawsuits that was still active from his pre-deceased ex-partner Augustus Herring. Despite spending his final years in Florida, Glenn H Curtiss was buried in his home town of Hammondsport where he was interred in the family plot at Pleasant Valley Cemetery.

While Glenn Curtiss received many awards and accolades during his lifetime, his memory was fully honoured in 1964 when he was inducted into the National Aviation Hall of Fame. His contribution to motorcycles was acknowledged in 1990, when he was inducted into the Motorsports' Hall of Fame of America, the Motorcycle Hall of Fame in 1998, and rounded off by the National Inventors' Hall of Fame in 2003.

Curtiss Early Pushers

The AEA machines

Although not Glenn Curtiss designs, the four aerodrome machines created by AEA included his design and development ideas. Aerodrome No.1 "Red Wing," was principally designed by Lt Thomas Selfridge. It was a biplane with an elevator ahead of the wings and a fixed fin/stabilizer behind. No.1 had no lateral control. Gaining its name because of the colour of its fabric, No.1 was first flown on March 12, 1908, and covered a distance of 318ft 11in before crash landing. The second flight, six days later, saw the aircraft crash after just 40yds because of the lack of lateral control.

The second aircraft, Aerodrome No.2 "White Wing," was sponsored by FW Baldwin. Very similar to the Red Wing, this aircraft featured lateral-control surfaces on all four wingtips, which would become more familiarly known as ailerons. Designed by Curtiss, lateral control was initiated by a yoke that embraced the pilot's shoulders, the turn being performed by leaning towards the desired direction. The first of four flights was carried out on May 18, 1908, the longest lasting for 339yds, with Curtiss at the controls.

The next aircraft was the Curtiss-sponsored Aerodrome No.3 "June Bug," which was a further refinement of the White Wing. First flown on June 21, 1908, the June Bug carried out a large number of flights including the first "leg" of the Scientific American Trophy, which called for a straight flight of one kilometre (3,281ft). Curtiss flew the leg with little difficulty, in fact, he continued for more than

The Curtiss "Hudson Flyer," which in the hands of Glenn Curtiss, bagged the $10,000 prize put up by the *New York World* newspaper to fly from Albany to New York City in May 1910.

The first Curtiss production aircraft was the Model D, which was priced from $3,500 to £5,000 with three different engines. The designations Model A to C cannot be applied to any Curtiss design.

one mile at an average speed of 39mph. Later renamed the "Loon," No.3 was fitted with a pair of large wooden pontoons but the hydrodynamic drag caused by the big floats combined with a lack of power would not release the Loon from the water.

The final AEA machine was Aerodrome No. 4, "Silver Dart," which was not as famous as the June Bug but was the most successful flying machine. Sponsored by a JAD McCurdy, the June Bug was powered by a 50hp Curtiss water-cooled V8 engine that drove the propeller with a chain and sprocket system. First flown by McCurdy on December 6, 1908, the aircraft later became the first of its kind to fly in Canada on February 29, 1909.

The first Curtiss aircraft

Ordered by the Aeronautical Society of New York on March 2, 1909, the first independent Curtiss design was the Curtiss No.1 "Gold Bug" (later "Golden Flyer"). It sold for $5,000, which included flight training of two society members. The Gold Bug was never included in the inventory of the company, despite being produced after the Herring-Curtiss period. The Aeronautical Society of New York wanted a representative in the 1909 Gordon Bennett Cup Race, in France, in August 1909, and for the society Curtiss built a bigger version of the Gold Bug. Named the "Reims Racer," the aircraft was powered by a 60hp V-8 engine. Curtiss flew the 20km circuit against the clock in a world record speed of 43.35mph.

The next challenge Curtiss set was to win a $10,000 prize put up by the *New York World Newspaper* for a flight between Albany, New York State, and New York City. The aircraft, named

One Model E was modified into a triplane but was fitted with a monoplane's forward elevator.

One of three Model Es supplied to the US Army in 1910 was No.6, originally fitted with a 40hp and rigged as a single, rather than two-seater. All pusher aircraft were grounded by the US Army in February 1914.

Aviator Ruth Law learned to fly in a Wright airplane, which featured double-handed controls as pictured, and as such could not make the transition to a Curtiss system. Therefore, her Model D was custom-built with Wright controls.

the "Hudson Flyer," was modified with normal wheeled undercarriage and emergency flotation gear. After one refuelling stop and once precautionary stop, Curtiss carried out the 156-mile flight on May 29, 1910.

A single aircraft, called the "Beachy Special," was built for Lincoln Beachey in 1911 before Curtiss began to start building the first of many production machines. The first of these was the single-seat Model D, which was marketed with three different engines including 40, 60 and 75hp, and the Model E, a two-seat variant with the same range of engines. The US Army and US Navy bought 12 examples of the Model D and E during 1911 and 1912; these pioneering machines later lead to the JN series.

Curtiss Early Seaplanes

The first time that Curtiss became involved with floatplanes was when Aerodrome No.3, renamed the Loon, was fitted with a pair of ungainly cloth-covered pontoons in 1908. Unsurprisingly, it would not fly from the water. By mid-1910, Curtiss had achieved some success in a Type III pusher fitted with a canoe, which was landed on Lake Keuka, New York, but had little chance of taking off again. In 1911, the concept was advanced further with the "Hydro," a pusher biplane that sat on a single main float with a forward float and a hydrofoil under the forward elevator. First flown on January 26, 1911, the aircraft was soon modified with a single 12ft-long main float with smaller balancer floats under each wingtip. This machine was followed by the Curtiss Tractor Hydro and the Triad, the latter being the world's first successful amphibian.

Attention was then turned to the flying-boat as a basic type, beginning with Flying-Boat No.1, which was fitted with a large pontoon under the lower wings. This was followed by Flying-Boat No.2, the Flying Fish, in 1912. This aircraft dictated the configuration of the basic biplane flying-boat for the next three decades and, for the first time, incorporated a hydrodynamic step into the under-surface of the hull, which was the key to successfully taking off from water. Following the Flying Fish, a series of experimental flying-boats appeared, culminating in the Type F, later known as the Model MF (Model 18 (M of MF = Modernized)), which was the only one to enter full production. The definitive Model F was sold to the US Army and US Navy and a number of civilian owners. The type evolved over several years, although it was the earlier models that sold in numbers to foreign air arms including the Russian Navy, which operated the type in the Baltic

One of many rapid developments of the Curtiss Model F was the FL, which used the wings from a Model L.

and Black seas, and the Italian Navy, which also flew eight examples license-built by Zari, based at Bovisio, Lombardy.

Other early flying-boats included the Judson Triplane (Model 7), a one-off for Mr Judson, and the Model K. The latter was a larger version of the Model F that first appeared in 1916 and, although not that successful in the US, it was widely exported. Curtiss also produced the Freak Boat in 1912, later sold to the US Navy as the C-1 (later AB-1); this aircraft performed the first successful catapult launch of a flying-boat.

The Curtiss "Hydro" or "Hydroaeroplane" was the first successful Curtiss seaplane design. First flown in January 1911, the aircraft featured tandem floats and a forward hydrovane.

The Curtiss Tractor Hydro was a modified Type III with engine forward and pilot aft. Glenn Curtiss was not happy with sitting in the slipstream or in line with the engine fumes.

Technical data – Model F (1917)	
ENGINE	One 100hp Curtiss OXX-3
WINGSPAN	45ft 1¼in
LENGTH	27ft 9¾in
WING AREA	387sq/ft
EMPTY WEIGHT	1,860lb
MAX TAKE-OFF WEIGHT	2,460lb
MAX SPEED	68mph
CEILING	4,500ft
ENDURANCE	5hrs 30mins

The world's first successful amphibian was the Triad, being demonstrated here by Curtiss at San Diego in February 1911.

In June 1911, Curtiss handed an example of a Model E to the US Navy, which designated the aircraft as the A-1 (later AH-1). The US Navy went on to buy 13 A-1s from Curtiss.

A Curtiss Tractor Hydro with a third wing, which could generate an additional 200lbs of lift.

Miscellaneous Types

Prolific builders of aircraft

Curtiss built a large number of one-off designs of his own, as well as special commissions for customers. Up to 1912, the configuration of choice was Pusher, but the appearance of the Model G Tractor set the tone for the future. Only two were built, both of them purchased by the US Army Signal Corps in 1913. Serialled No.21 and 22, the former was a side-by-side two-seater with a tricycle undercarriage powered by a 75hp Curtiss O, while the latter had a quadri-cycle undercarriage and a 90hp engine.

In 1917, the conundrum of combining an airplane and a car began with the Model 11 Autoplane, complete with detachable wings. A flying lifeboat was also built in the same year; the Model BT could jettison its wings and empennage after landing in the sea. Curtiss took on the challenge of replacing the excellent Bristol F.2B by producing the Model CB Battleplane powered by a Liberty engine, while the Model HA (Model 16) floatplane was designed by Capt BL Smith. The Model 16 appeared as the HA-1 and HA-2 fighters, the latter with redesigned wings for service with the United States Marine Corps (USMC). A single Model HA Mail landplane evolved in 1919.

The Curtiss L (Model 9) was a triplane that first appeared in 1916 and was intended as a side-by-side trainer for the private flyer. Powered by a 90hp OX, one Model L-1 was built with a modified tail and revised interplane struts, and four more as the L-2 with a 100hp engine, OXX engine and floats.

One Curtiss Model HA-2 was built and only differed from the HA-2 in having revised wings.

One of many attempts to create a flying car, the Model 11 Autoplane first appeared in 1917. It is pictured on May 2, 1917, minus all detachable flying surfaces.

The Model S was a widely developed small scout, built as a single S-1 Speed Scout in 1916. One Model S-2 Wireless without bracing wires was built, as well as four Model S-3 (Model 10) triplanes, a single S-4 (Model 10A) with twin floats (the first of its kind to be built by Curtiss,) and one Model S-5 (Model 10B) float triplane with a single main float and a pair of outboard sponsons. One Model S-6 (Model 10C) was also built, which was an improved version of the S-3, installed with two machine guns rather than one.

The largest aircraft to be built by Curtiss, to date, was the Model T (Model 3) Wanamaker (Rodman Wanamaker was the inspiration for the original Model H), which was constructed on behalf of Wanamaker in 1916. The world's largest aircraft, at the time, with a wingspan of 134ft, the aircraft was powered by four 240hp Renault in-line engines. Twenty were ordered by the Royal Naval Air Service (RNAS), but only the prototype was ever received and the remaining 19 were cancelled.

Designed by Charles Kirkham around his own 400hp K-12 engine, the Model 18T series was a triplane fighter. The fighter was developed into a number of designs, including the Model 18T-1 Wasp

An attempt to produce an American version of the highly successful Bristol F.2B Fighter, the Model CB Battleplane was powered by a Liberty engine but was wrecked during early flight testing.

Built in Canada, the C-1 Canada used the flying surfaces of the H-4 flying-boat, combined with a short landplane fuselage.

prototype with short-span wings and the Model 18T-2 with longer-span wings capable of being fitted with wheeled undercarriage or floats. There was also the Model 18B Hornet (Model 15A), two of which saw service with the US Army, while the 18T-1s saw post-war service with both the US Army and the US Navy in a number of high-speed trials and races.

One Model E was modified into a triplane but was fitted with a monoplane's forward elevator.

With no interplane bracing, the Curtiss Model S-2 was named the "Wireless."

JN-2 and 3

Development

The famous line of Curtiss JN aircraft was actually an amalgamation of two designs, the Model J and the Model N. The former was designed by Englishman, BD Thomas, who used to work for Sopwith. Only two Model Js were built but they achieved some fame by becoming the fastest American aircraft, at 85.7mph, in September 1914 and raising the altitude record to 17,441ft on October 8. The Model N was developed at the same time, and it would evolve into the successful N-9 seaplane. The sole Model N featured an 100hp OXX engine, improved wings and a top speed of 82mph. It was from these two aircraft that the first Model JN emerged, effectively becoming the first "Jenny."

Design

The Curtis JN was actually ordered as the Model J Modified but when it was received by the US Army, the designation JN-2 was applied (JN-1 was never used.) Fitted with equal-span wings with an Eiffel 36 aerofoil, the JN-2 had ailerons fitted to both the upper and lower mainplanes. The ailerons were connected by struts and controlled by a shoulder-yoke system, which was destined to be unpopular with military pilots.

JN-2s in service were progressively modified, (including the fitment of the OXX engine) to the point where they were redesignated as the JN-3. The final versions of the JN-3 had unequal-span wings and ailerons fitted to the upper mainplane only. The control system was improved to feature a more traditional control wheel for the ailerons and a foot-bar for the rudder.

Service

Ordered by the US Army in December 1914, the first JN-2s joined the 1st Aero Squadron, Aviation Section, US Signal Corps, under the command of Capt TD Milling, by July 1915. The following month, the unit moved to Fort Sill, Oklahoma, for manoeuvres with the Field Artillery School. It then moved to the Mexican border in March 1916, where the JN-2s became the first US Army aircraft to be

The first of eight JN-2s ordered by the US Army in December 1914, serialled No.41. The aircraft was wrecked while trying to land at night at Pearson, New Mexico, on March 19, 1916.

involved in tactical operations. One pilot was killed and a second aircraft was wrecked before the JN-2s began to be modified into the more capable JN-3.

In early 1915, 91 JN-3s were ordered for the RNAS, which was by far the largest operator of the type, though the service only existed until early 1917 in a variety of roles from early home defence to training. Following the upgrade of the surviving JN-2s to JN-3 standard, the US Army ordered two more of the latter before the arrival of the definitive JN-4.

Production

Two Model Js, one Model N, eight JN-2s, serialled 41–48 and 99 JN-3s were produced by Curtiss; 91 of the latter were purchased for the RNAS and serialled 1362–67 and 3345–423. Twelve JN-3s were built in a branch factory in Toronto, serialled 8392–403, and two JN-3s in US Army service were serialled 52 and 53.

Technical data – JN-2 and JN-3	
ENGINE	(JN-2) One 90hp Curtiss OX; (JN-3) one 100hp Curtiss OXX
WINGSPAN	40ft 2in
LENGTH	26ft 8in
WING AREA	340sq/ft
EMPTY WEIGHT	1,270lb
MAX TAKE-OFF WEIGHT	1,675lb
MAX SPEED	75mph
ENDURANCE	4hrs, with pilot only
ARMAMENT	Two fixed and one or two flexibly mounted 0.3in machine-guns, plus one 500lb or two 116lb underwing bombs

The Canadian-built prototype JN.3, 8392, after it was repaired by Fairey, effectively bringing the aircraft up to JN.4 standard. The aircraft was known as the JN.3 (Improved) and, after several scraps, the aircraft was destroyed when a wing came off in a dive on September 7, 1917. The pilot, TPFO J M Dawson, died of his injuries.

R-2 and R-3 (Model 2)

Development

By late 1914, Curtiss was expanding as an aircraft manufacturer and the company was attracting an increasing number of experienced staff, including designers with knowledge of tractor-powered aircraft. The company was keen to expand on the Model J and N for military use, and the result was a larger version of these aircraft, designated the Model R.

Design

A scaled-up version of the Model N, the Model R prototype, had equal-span stagger wings. It could be operated as either a land or floatplane in the military reconnaissance role, with a pilot and observer accommodated in one long open cockpit. The production version, the R-2, had unequal-span wings with ailerons fitted to the upper mainplane. The aircraft had a fixed fin with a horn-balanced rudder and the pilot and observer had widely spaced individual cockpits. The sole R-2A was completed first with equal span wings with the same style of cockpit as the production R-2. The two R-3 seaplanes differed from the R-2 by having wings of increased span to help bear the weight of the large twin floats.

Service

The Model R prototype first flew in early 1915, while the R-2 entered production later in the year. Twelve were sold to the US Army at $12,000 each, several of them seeing service with the Mexican Punitive Expedition. Serviceability of the R-2s in this theatre was not good, but many reconnaissance and liaison operations were successfully carried out.

In total, 100 R-2s were ordered for the RNAS in late 1915, although only 87 were delivered. The first, 3445, arrived at Hendon on December 24, 1915. Like the JN-3, all were built in Toronto and, as well as the original 160hp VX engine, several were delivered with the 'in service' 200hp Sunbeam Arab II installed. Several saw action in Northern France with 3 Wing and were in widespread use across Britain with a host of units, but the majority had been withdrawn by late 1917.

The R-2A, which was the first to fly, was used by Curtiss test pilot, Raymond V Morris, to set a new American altitude record for one pilot and three passengers in August 1915 and reached 8,105ft. The two R-3 seaplanes were purchased by the US Navy in 1916.

Production

Total production included one Model R prototype; 112 R-2s, 12 of which were for the US Army, serialled 64–75, and 100 (87) ordered for the Royal Flying Corp (RFC), serialled 3445–544 (3531–44 not delivered); one R-2A (Improved R) and two R-3 Floatplanes, serialled AH-62 and AH65 (later A66 and A67) for the US Navy.

Technical data – R-2	
ENGINE	One 160hp Curtiss V-X; (R-2 RFC) one 200hp Sunbeam Arab II
WINGSPAN	(R-2) 45ft 11½in; (R-3) 57ft 1in
LENGTH	38ft 4¾in
WING AREA	504.88sq/ft
EMPTY WEIGHT	1,822lb
MAX TAKE-OFF WEIGHT	3,092lb
MAX SPEED	86mph
CLIMB RATE	4,000ft in 10mins
ENDURANCE	6hrs 42mins

Delivered to Hendon, north London, on May 12, 1916, R-2 3449 is pictured during trials at Grain when the aircraft was part the Gunnery Experimental Unit. The aircraft remained on Royal Naval Air Service (RNAS) strength until March 1918.

R-4 (Model 2)

Development

An improved version of the R-2, the R-4 was difficult to distinguish from its predecessor and its performance was only marginally superior.

Design

The R-4 incorporated several minor modifications including increased structural strengthening, strut-connected ailerons and a redesigned, repositioned tail skid. A more powerful Curtiss V-2-3 piston engine was installed, which only gave a slight edge over the R-2.

By late 1917, several of the US Army and US Navy's bigger single-engine types became available as test beds, including one R-4. The aircraft was used to test a 400hp Liberty engine, and this was found to improve the characteristics to such a degree that 12 aircraft, designated R-4L, were ordered and several more were converted to Liberty power. Externally, the R-4L was distinguishable from the R-2 because of the enlarged nose radiator needed to cool the Liberty.

On May 15, 1918, the US Army was put in charge of the new US Air Mail service and at the time was operating several JN-4Hs. It was clear from an early stage that the load-carrying capability of the JN-4H was inadequate and, at the request of the US Army, Curtiss converted six R-4Ls to R-4LM standard. The conversion work centered on the front cockpit, which was adapted into a mail compartment with a capacity of 400lbs.

Service

The R-4 entered service with the US Army in 1916, several seeing action with General Pershing's Mexican Punitive Expedition against insurgents, led by Pancho Villa. Two more R-4s were built following the US entry into World War One, in July 1917. The same year, 12 Liberty-powered R-4Ls entered service, while the half dozen mail-carrying R-4LMs continued in service until early 1920.

Production

In total, 53 R-4s were ordered by the US Army in 1916 and were serialled 177–192, 218–316 and 469, 2157 and 37932. Another 12 R-4Ls were built, serialled 39362–67 and 39954–59, and several more were converted. Six R-4Ls were converted to R-4LM standard.

Technical data – R-4	
ENGINE	(R-4) One 200hp Curtiss V-2-3; (R-L and LM) one 400hp Liberty
WINGSPAN	48ft
LENGTH	28ft 11¾in
HEIGHT	13ft 2¼in
WING AREA	504.88sq/ft
EMPTY WEIGHT	2,275lb
MAX TAKE-OFF WEIGHT	3,242lb
MAX SPEED	90mph
CLIMB RATE	4,000ft in 10mins
MAX RANGE	350 miles

One of six R-4Ls converted to R-4LM for service as mail carriers. Note the blanked over forward cockpit, which served as a compartment for up to 400lb of mail.

H-4 to H-10 (Model 6/H series)

Development
The long, successful story of the Model H series of flying-boats began in 1914 when the US responded to a challenge set by the *Daily Mail*, which offered a £10,000 prize for the first non-stop crossing of the Atlantic.

Design
The original Model H "America" (retrospectively designated H-1) was a conventional two-bay biplane with a pair of tractor-mounted engines positioned above the fuselage between the wings. Very similar to earlier Curtiss designs, the Model H was much larger to accommodate enough fuel for an Atlantic crossing. In August 1914, as they were prepared for their journey across the Atlantic from Felixstowe, the two Model Hs were commandeered and subsequently purchased by the RNAS. Impressed with the aircraft, an order was placed for one H-2 and ultimately 64 H-4s, known as "Small Americas," powered by a pair of 90hp Curtiss OX water-cooled engines. These engines were later replaced by a pair of 100hp Clerget rotary air-cooled radials.

One example of a larger version of the H-4 was built as the H-8 and offered to the US Navy but instead was purchased by the Admiralty to serve as a pattern aircraft for the H-12. The H-10 was a twin-boomed Curtiss OX-powered flying-boat, and only one prototype was built.

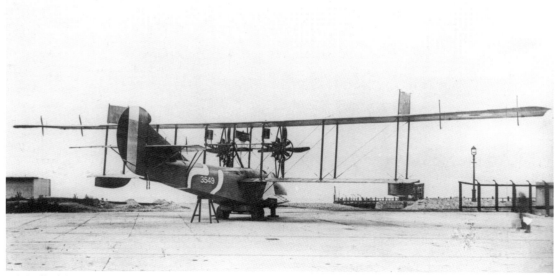

Originally delivered to Felixstowe in July 1915, H-4 3549 also served with the Felixstowe Seaplane School until August 1918. Note the large sponson on the lower sides of the forward fuselage/hall, which was added to stop the power of the engines digging the hull into the water during taxiing.

Service

The two H-1 Small America flying-boats were serialled 950 and 951 in RNAS service, both served at Felixstowe from October and November 1914, respectively. Many experimental modifications were applied to both aircraft and, by May 1916, both had been 'deleted' from service. The first H-4 Small America was delivered to Felixstowe in June 1915 and, by August, a few began to enter service with the Killingholme Seaplane School and later with the Felixstowe Seaplane School. Several H-4s were delivered to Felixstowe but were destined not to leave their packing cases. Several H-4s were shipped to Gibraltar and Malta and from there they were employed on maritime patrol and reconnaissance operations. A large proportion of the H-4 fleet had been withdrawn from service by 1917, but at least one remained in use for trials and experimental modifications until 1919.

Production

Total production included two H-1 Small Americas, serialled 950 and 951; 62 H-4 Small Americas, ordered on December 23, 1915, and serialled 1228–35, 1236–39 and 3545–94, the last batch being built in Toronto; one H-8 and one H-10 prototype. Another eight H-4s were built by Airco and Saunders.

Technical data – H-4 and H-8	
ENGINE	(H-4) two 90hp Curtiss OX-5, or for the RNAS two 100hp Anzani or two 130hp Clerget; (H-8) two 160hp Curtiss, later 250hp Rolls-Royce Eagle VIII
WINGSPAN	(upper) 74ft
EMPTY WEIGHT	3,000lb
LOADED WEIGHT	5,000lb
MAX SPEED	146mph at sea level
SERVICE CEILING	16,250ft
MAX RANGE	720 miles
ARMAMENT	Two fixed and one or two flexibly mounted 0.3in machine-guns and one 500lb or two 116lb underwing bombs

The sole Curtiss H-10, a slightly larger version of the H-8, with thin twin booms, which ran from the rear of the Curtiss OX engines to the tailplane.

Curtiss H-4 "Small America" 3592 at Felixstowe after a pair of Anzani engines were fitted in September 1917. The aircraft served the Felixstowe Seaplane School until August 1918.

JN-4

Development

One of the most significant American-built aircraft of its day, the JN-4, affectionately nicknamed the Jenny, saw widespread military and civilian service into the 1930s. When the US entered World War One, 95 percent of all military pilots in America and Canada trained on the type. Post-World War One, thousands of examples flooded on to the civilian market, where they became well known as the barnstormer of choice in the many traveling air shows that traversed the US.

Design

The original JN-4 was virtually identical to the JN-3, complete with unequal-span, two-bay wings and a cross-axle main undercarriage. The JN-4A was a refined variant with a larger tailplane, revised fuselage lines, increased dihedral wings and six degrees of down-thrust for the engine. The JN-4B was an older design than the JN-4A and had a level mounted OX-2 engine, ailerons on the upper mainplane and an uncut upper centre section. The JN-4 "Canuck," built in Canada, followed, featuring a metal tail assembly, strut-connected ailerons and a stick-type control system. The prolific JN-4D, built by seven different US aircraft manufacturers (including Curtiss) had stick control and the same downward-thrust as the JN-4A. The JN-4H was fitted with an 150hp Hispano-Suiza for advanced trainer performance. Dual-control, bomber trainer and gunnery trainer variants of the JN-4H all saw service. One JN-5H was built but this led to the JN-6, which was an improved version of the JN-4H. Once again, a wide range of multi-role sub-variants were produced.

Service

The early JN-4s first appeared in July 1916, and the majority went on to serve with RNAS and RFC but the US Army only placed a tentative order. The JN-4A first appeared in November 1916 and, once again, the type served the RNAS and RFC, but this time, 601 were bought by the US Army. When the JN-4B first appeared, it was still pre-war America and sales to civilian customers were gaining momentum. The Canadian-built Canuck arrived in January 1917, and 680 of the 1,260 built were supplied to the US Army; the remainder to the Canadian Air Force, several of which served with Canadian flying schools operating in Texas. The JN-4D appeared as the US entered World War One, and as such, large numbers were ordered; deliveries took place between November 1917 and January 1919.

The JN-4 was retired by the Canadians in 1924 and the US Army was winding up its fleet by 1926, and many surplus aircraft were sold for as little as $50 each in their original packing crate. However, in civilian hands, the type remained a common sight until the early 1930s.

Production

Total JN-4/5 and 6 production was more than 7,000 aircraft comprising 130 JN-4s, 781 JN-4As, 76 JN-4Bs, two JN-4cs, 1,260 JN-4 Canucks, 2812 JN-4Ds, one JN-4D-2, 929 JN-4Hs, one JN-5H, and 1,035 JN-6 Improved JN-4H. Manufacturers involved in Jenny production were Curtiss; Fowler Airplane Co, San Francisco; Liberty Iron Works, Sacramento; Springfield Aircraft Co, Sacramento; St Louis Aircraft Co, St Louis; US Aircraft Corp, Redwood City; Howell and Lesser Co, San Francisco; and Canadian Aeroplanes Ltd.

Technical data – JN-4D	
ENGINE	One 90hp Curtiss OX-5
WINGSPAN	43ft 7¾in
LENGTH	27ft 4in
HEIGHT	9ft 10½in
WING AREA	352sq/ft
EMPTY WEIGHT	1,390lb
MAX TAKE-OFF WEIGHT	1,920lb
MAX SPEED	75mph
SERVICE CEILING	6,500ft

Right: The Curtiss JN-4 "Jenny" has appeared in many films over the years, including the 1957 picture *The Spirit of St Louis*, starring James Stewart as Charles Lindbergh.

Below: The JN-4 was popular with private flyers and barnstorming acts but also with post-war flying schools. This aircraft, in service with a school at Rich Field, Waco, Texas, proudly boasts just one fatality in 4,000 hours of flying.

N-9 (Model 5)

Development
Effectively a floatplane version of the JN-4B Jenny, the N-9 quickly established itself as the standard US Navy primary trainer of the late World War One period and into the early 1920s.

Design
The N-9 drew heavily from the key design features of the JN-4 but featured a large central float, wingtip sponson floats and a lengthened centre section. The span was increased by inserting an extra center section in the upper wing and 5ft lower-wing extensions on each side of the fuselage to help cope with the extra weight of the floats. The ailerons fitted to the upper mainplane were enlarged.

Power was provided by an 100hp Curtiss OXX for the N-9, which was slightly underpowered. When replaced by the more able 150hp Wright A (a license-built Hispano-Suiza), the more powerful machine was designated as the N-9H, while the 100hp models were designated retrospectively as the N-9C. The N-9H featured a large spinner, and in place of a large frontal radiator, a large vertical radiator was mounted above the fuselage in front of the leading edge.

Service
An initial contract for 30 N-9s was placed by the US Navy in August 1916 and there was an additional order for 14 aircraft, serialled 433–446, by the US Army. The total order quickly grew to 560 aircraft; the US Navy being the primary customer, as the N-9 had been deemed suitable as a primary seaplane trainer. The first entered service in 1917. The N-9 saw extensive service in all of the US Navy's training establishments and, by the time the type was withdrawn in 1927, more than 2,500 pilots had trained with the type.

The N-9 also pioneered new flying techniques, which are still taught today, thanks the efforts of USMC pilot, FT Evans. It was while disproving the theory that an N-9 could not be looped that Evans

One of the last Curtiss-built N-9Cs, A-365, delivered to the US Navy pictured at Naval Air Station (NAS) Pensacola in 1918.

discovered the tried-and-tested method of recovery from spin by releasing back-pressure and applying opposite rudder to the direction of the spin followed by recovery from the ensuing dive.

Production

In total, 560 N-9s were ordered by the US Navy; only 100 of these were built by Curtiss, the remainder by the Curtiss-owned subsidiary, Burgess & Co, based at Marblehead, Massachusetts. Curtiss-built N-9Cs were serialled A60–65, A85–90, A201–234, A294–301 and A342–373; and Curtiss-built N-9Hs were serialled A2286–2290. Burgess-built N-9Cs were serialled A409–438, A999–1028 and A2351–2409; and N-9Hs were serialled A2410–2572 and A2574–2650. Fifty N-9Hs assembled at Naval Air Station (NAS) Pensacola were serialled A6528–6542, A6618–33, A6733–42 and A7091–100.

Technical data – N9-C and N9-H	
ENGINE	(N-9C) One 100hp Curtiss OXX-3; (N-9H) one 150hp wright A
WINGSPAN	53ft 4in
LENGTH	(N-9C) 29ft 10in; (N-9H) 30ft 10in
HEIGHT	(N-9C) 10ft 10½in; (N-9H) 10ft 11in
WING AREA	496sq/ft
EMPTY WEIGHT	(N-9C) 1,860lb; (N-9H) 2,140lb
GROSS WEIGHT	(N-9C) 2,410lb; (N-9H) 2,750lb
MAX SPEED	(N-9C) 70mph; (N-9H) 78mph
CLIMB RATE	(N-9C) 2,000ft in 10min; (N-9H) 3,240ft in 10mins
MAX RANGE	(N-9C) 200 miles
CEILING	(N-9H) 6,600ft
ARMAMENT	Two fixed and one or two flexibly mounted 0.3in machine-guns and one 500lb bomb

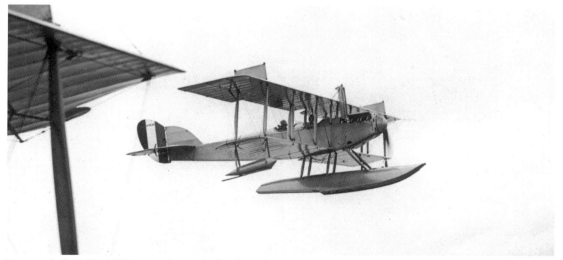

Burgess-built N-9H, A2524; note the vertical radiator, large spinner and stabilizing fins above the upper mainplane, all key features of the H model.

H-12 and H-16 (Model 6A-D)

Development

Both developments of the H-4 (Model 6), the H-12 and H-16 "Large America" flying-boats were the most successful of the H-series, and both variants remained in US Navy service until the late 1920s. The biggest and most powerful (once re-engined) to see operational service during World War One were the Large Americas, and they gave the RAF and US Navy an excellent maritime reconnaissance capability.

Design

The H-12 was an unequal-span three-bay biplane with a side-by-side cockpit forward of the wings for the pilot and co-pilot, protected by a large, curved windscreen with a glazed roof. Observer/gunner positions were located at the bow and midships, all of which were armed with 0.303in Lewis machine guns. The Curtiss engines were strut-mounted below the upper mainplane so that they were clear of spray during take-off and landing.

Originally powered by Curtiss engines, the H-12 performed well enough but both the British and US Navy thought that the flying-boats were underpowered. The British re-engined their aircraft with the 275hp Eagle I and later with the 375hp eagle VIII, while the US Navy upgraded to the 360hp Liberty.

The H-16 (Model 6C) was a direct development of the H-12 but still had its roots in the original H-4. Slightly larger than its predecessor, the H-16 featured a revised hull and stronger structure with power provided by a pair of Liberty engines for the US Navy and the Eagle IV for the RAF. The many that remained in post-war service with the US Navy were re-engined with 400 Liberty 12A engines and incorporated components from the F-5L.

Service

The H-12 first flew in late 1916 and by the beginning of 1917, the type was in service with the RNAS and the US Navy. The RNAS, later RAF, H-12s played a crucial role in suppressing U-boat menace around the coast of Britain and Ireland right up to the Armistice. The US Navy H-12s were kept at home and a few remained in service until the late 1920s, while the RAF had retired its aircraft by mid-1919.

Curtiss H-12 8670 was one of several Large Americas that carried out attacks on U-boats around the British coast. One 230lb bomb was dropped on a U-boat off in October 1917 and two 230lbs on a U-boat south of the Needles, Isle of Wight, the following month.

First flown in March 1918, the H-16 was in service with the RAF's 230, 234, 240 and 257 Squadrons by August. Unlike the H-12, the US Navy deployed its H-16s to the European theatre and several served alongside RAF machines before the Armistice. Unlike the RAF, which retired its H-16s from squadron service in June 1919, the US Navy retained the type until May 1930.

Production

In total, 104 H-12s (Model 6As) were built, 84 for the RNAS and 20 (Model 6Bs) for the US Navy. H-16 (Model 6C) comprised 334 aircraft, of which 184 were built by Curtiss and 150 by the Naval Aircraft Factory in Philadelphia.

Technical data – H-12A and H-16	
ENGINE	(Proto) Two 160hp Curtiss V-X-X; (H-12) two 200hp Curtiss V-2-3; (H-12A) two 275hp Rolls-Royce Eagle I or two 375hp Eagle VIII; (H-16) two 360hp Liberty or two 345hp Eagle IV or two 400hp Liberty 12A
WINGSPAN	(H-12) 92ft 8½in; (H-16) 95ft 0¾in
LENGTH	(H-12) 46ft 6in; (H-16) 46ft 1½in
HEIGHT	(H-12) 16ft 6in; (H-16) 17ft 8¾in
WING AREA	(H-12) 1,216sq/ft; (H-16) 1,164sq/ft
EMPTY WEIGHT	(H-12) 7,293lb; (H-16) 7,400lb
MAX TAKE-OFF WEIGHT	(H-12) 10,650lb; (H-16) 10,900lb
MAX SPEED	(H-12) 85mph; (H-16) 95mph at sea level
SERVICE CEILING	(H-12) 10,800ft; (H-16) 9,950ft
ENDURANCE	(H-12) 6hrs
RANGE	(H-16) 378 miles
ARMAMENT	(H-12) Four 0.303in Lewis machine guns in twin bow and midships mountings, plus up to 460lb of bombs on underwing racks; (H-16) six 0.303in Lewis machine guns, plus up to 920lb of bombs

An unidentified Curtiss H-16 warms through its 345hp Rolls-Royce Eagle IV engines at Killingholme, Lincolnshire, in 1918.

R-6, R-7 and R-9 (Model 2A)

Development
A two-seat torpedo-bomber reconnaissance floatplane, the R-6 was a longer span version of the R-3 with more powerful engines. Built for the US Army and US Navy, it was the latter that exploited the aircraft the most, its long range proving to be a particularly useful asset.

Design
All but one of the 76 R-6s ordered by the US Navy had twin floats; the exception being A193, which was experimentally fitted with a single float and outer wing sponsons. For the US army, several R-6s were ordered as landplanes but the bulk of these were later transferred to the navy and fitted with floats.

The R-6L differed in its engine, a 360hp inline low-compression piston, while the sole R-7 was powered by a 200hp Curtiss V-2-3 as used by the R-4. The R-7 was a landplane and because of the strut configuration, the aircraft appeared to have its roots more in the R-3 than the R-6.

The R-9 was a dedicated bomber variant of the R-6 with controls repositioned so that the pilot flew the aircraft from the front cockpit, while the observer/bombardier carried out his duties from the rear.

Service
Out of sequence, the first of this group of aircraft to fly was the R-7 in late 1916. Curtiss test pilot Victor Carlstrom attempted to fly from Chicago to New York City non-stop for the first time in November 1916 but failed at approximately the half-way point. Cut short by a fuel leak, the flight was still a US non-stop record, as the R-7 had covered 452 miles.

The most common configuration of the R-6 was the twin-float arrangement for the US Navy, although this example is one of only 18 R-6s to serve with the US Army.

The R-6 entered US Navy service in 1917, destined to become the first US-built aircraft to serve overseas when a squadron was sent to the Azores in January 1918 for maritime patrol duties. The R-6L began to appear in 1918, and in 1920 several became involved in the US Navy's rekindled interest in aerial-torpedo dropping. A number of R-6Ls later served operationally as torpedo-bombers until they were replaced by more modern machines; the last R-6Ls having been retired by 1926.

The R-9 was in US Army and US Navy service by early 1918 and was withdrawn by the early 1920s unless converted to R-6L standard, after which many served on until 1929.

Production

In total, 76 R-6s were ordered for the US Navy, serialled A162–197 and A302–341; a further 18 were ordered by the US Army, serialled 504–521, although most of these are believed to have been diverted to the Navy. Forty R-6Ls were converted from R-6s in 1918 and another 14 were converted from R-9s. One R-7 and 112 R-9s were ordered for the US Navy, serialled A873–984, and ten for the US Army, serialled 39033–42.

Technical data – R-6L	
ENGINE	(R-6) One 200hp V-2-3; (R-6L) one 360hp Liberty
WINGSPAN	57ft 1¼in
LENGTH	33ft 5in
HEIGHT	14ft 2in
WING AREA	613sq/ft
EMPTY WEIGHT	3,513lb
MAX TAKE-OFF WEIGHT	4,634lb
MAX SPEED	100mph
SERVICE CEILING	12,200ft
RANGE	565 miles
ARMAMENT	One 1,036lb torpedo

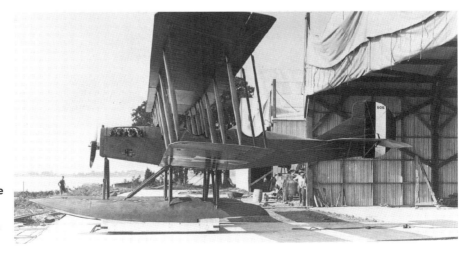

The second R-6 to be delivered to the US Army, serialled 505. A purposeful looking aircraft, the majority of the US Army R-6s were later transferred to the US Navy.

A Liberty-powered R-6L with engine fully exposed, with its pilot (centre) and observer (left); the latter with an aerial camera.

Model GS

Development

The first Curtiss design to be constructed from the outset with a rotary engine, the Gnome Scout (GS) was built as a seaplane. In 1917, the US Navy placed an order for five single-seat seaplane biplane scouts, which were subsequently amended to six aircraft when a request was made to supply one machine as a triplane. Despite being at the end of the order, the sole triplane was designated as GS-1 and the five biplanes as the GS-2.

Design

Beginning with the GS-1, the design owed much to the earlier Curtiss S-3 (Model 10) and S-4 (Model 10A) triplane seaplanes. The GS-1 attempted to deal with the problem of how uncomfortable a seaplane was to operate during choppy water take off and landing. Up to that time, seaplanes had their floats attached to the lower fuselage by a rigid mount or truss. However, the GS-1 featured shock absorbers within the struts that were attached from the main central float to the fuselage. On paper, the idea seemed good but in practise the rigging flexed, causing a change in the trim angle of the float at speed on the water, resulting in an even more uncomfortable 'porpoising' effect. The GS-1 was nicknamed the 'Flying Door Knob Control' by Curtiss test pilots because of an overly complex carburation control for the engine.

The GS-2 appeared, on the surface, to be a biplane version of the GS-1 but was, in fact, a completely different design. How they differed is not recorded and all of the technical details are lacking, other than that both were powered by a 100hp Gnome rotary engine.

One of only a few grainy snapshots of the GS-1 known to exist, showing flight testing by a Curtiss test pilot.

Service

The GS-1 was delivered to the US Navy in Florida on January 1, 1918, and was destined to have a short career. Following a thorough demonstration of the GS-1 by a Curtiss pilot, the aircraft was handed over to a US Navy acceptance pilot who, after a few flights, wrecked the aircraft beyond repair after a very heavy landing on April 1.

The first of five GS-2s, A445, was accepted by the US Navy on February 14, 1918, and the last, A449, was delivered on August 9. Little more is known about the careers of these elusive seaplanes other than A447 was sold off in August 1920 and A449 was struck off charge (SOC) from US Navy service in November 1923.

Production

Six aircraft, in total, were manufactured, comprising one GS-1 triplane serialled A868 and five GS-2 biplanes, serialled A445–449.

The first Curtiss aircraft to be designed with a rotary engine, three of the five GS-2s are pictured at an advanced stage of their construction.

NC-1 to 4 Flying-Boat (Model 12)

Development

Working closely with Glenn Curtiss in 1917, the US Navy requested that the company design and build a flying-boat capable of crossing the Atlantic. The idea was for the aircraft to be in a suitable condition to start operations soon after arrival, rather than being delivered in a crate. Four flying-boats were ordered, prefixed with "NC" which stood for Navy-Curtiss.

Design

The NC flying-boats were wide-span biplanes, initially designed with three tractor engines. The hull was relatively short, almost half the length of the span, but could accommodate a crew of five with the pilots in an open cockpit. A large biplane tail structure was supported by long booms that projected from the trailing edge of the wing and from the rear of the hull. Once the design was submitted to the navy, an order for four aircraft was placed with Curtiss, along with six more to be built by the Naval Aircraft Factory.

The first aircraft, designated NC-1, was configured as per the original design, but had to be modified with a fourth Liberty engine because it did not have enough power to carry the fuel it needed to cross the Atlantic. NC-2 had the centre Liberty mounted as a pusher but was reconfigured to four engines installed in tandem pairs. NC-3 had a four-engine layout from the outset, as did NC-4, both receiving the benefit of the flight development trials of the first two aircraft.

Service

NC-1 made its maiden flight on October 4, 1918, in the hands of Cdr Richardson who, in the following month, set a new record when 51 passengers plus crew were carried. NC-2 first flew in February 1919, but was later wrecked after the flying-boat was blown ashore during a storm. NC-3 and NC-4 first flew in April 1919 in preparation for their epic flight the following month.

On May 16, 1919, NC-1, NC-3 and NC-4 took off from Trepassey Bay, Newfoundland, to carry out the first leg of the transatlantic crossing to Horta in the Azores. NC-1 and NC-3 never made it, but NC-4, commanded by Lt Cdr AC Read, continued on. After further stops at Ponta, Delgada, Lisbon and Ferrol del Caudillo, NC-4 landed in Plymouth Sound, UK, on May 31. The NC-4 entered the record books by becoming the first aircraft to cross the Atlantic but unfortunately for the crew their feat was eclipsed by John Alcock and Arthur Brown's non-stop flight on June 14 and 15, 1919.

Donated to the Smithsonian Institute, NC-4 is on display in the National Museum of Naval Aviation, Pensacola, Florida.

Production

One NC-1 A2291, one NC-2 A2292, one NC-3 A2293 and one NC-4 A2294 were built at Garden City, New York, with final assembly carried out at NAS Rockway. Six NCs, which were to be built by the Naval Aircraft Factory, were cancelled after the Armistice.

Technical data – NC-4	
ENGINE	Four 400hp Liberty 12A
WINGSPAN	126ft
LENGTH	68ft 3in
HEIGHT	24ft 5in
WING AREA	2,441sq/ft
EMPTY WEIGHT	16,000lb
MAX TAKE-OFF WEIGHT	28,000lb
MAX SPEED	85mph
SERVICE CEILING	2,500ft
ENDURANCE	14hrs 45mins at cruising speed
ARMAMENT	Two 0.30in machine guns, one fixed and one flexible

The only surviving NC flying-boat, NC-4 A2294, during a goodwill tour of the US East Coast, following the successful Atlantic crossing by Lt Cdr Read and his crew.

HS-1, 2 and 3 (Model 8)

Development
The story of the HS (Model 8) series of successful flying-boats began with the H-14, which was a smaller version of the H-12, with a pair of pusher engines as per the original H-1 America. The US Army placed an order for 16 H-4s but after the prototype was flown, the order was cancelled because of poor performance. Not to be outdone, the Curtiss engineers reconfigured the H-14 with a single, more powerful engine and the HS series was born.

Design
The HS-1 comprised a single-step hull with a wide planing bottom and lateral sponsons with three-bay unequal span wings. The crew of two or three comprised an observer/gunner in a bow cockpit armed with a pair of Lewis machine guns and a pilot and/or co-pilot in a side-by-side cockpit, in front of the leading edge of the lower mainplane.

Power for the prototype was a 200hp Curtiss V-X-3 but the first production model was propelled by a 360hp Liberty. The production HS-1L also featured horn-balanced ailerons and two degrees of dihedral in the outer sections of the wings. The desire to carry a larger offensive load brought about the HS-2L, which had a 74ft 1in span, which increased the wing area and gave the flying-boat more lift. As a result, the HS-2L could carry a pair of 230lb depth charges, which were far more effective than the 180lb charges carried by the HS-1L. A few redesigned HS-3s with a new hull, fin and rudder were built but the design was shelved when the Armistice was announced.

Service
The first HS-1Ls were received by the US Navy in late 1917 and the type fully entered service in early 1918, mainly for anti-submarine duties along the eastern coast of the US and the Panama Canal. The first of many HS flying-boats joined US Navy units in France from May 1918 and they were destined to see considerable service flying coastal patrol, convoy escort and anti-submarine operations until the end of the war.

Post-war, many HSs were sold as surplus as the US Navy began a rapid contraction, although a number did remain in service as patrol aircraft and trainers until 1928. The United States Coast Guard used 11 HSs until 1926 and several remained airworthy in private hands until the early 1930s in the US and Canada.

Production
In total, 1,117 HS flying-boats were delivered to the US Navy between 1917 and 1919. Of these, 675 HS-1L/HS-2Ls were built by Curtiss; 250 HS-1L/HS-2Ls by Lowe, Willard & Fowler (LWF); 80 HS-2Ls by Standard; 60 HS-2Ls by Gallaudet; 25 HS-2Ls by Boeing; two HS-2Ls by Lougheed; and 25 HS-2Ls assembled by the US Navy from spare parts. Six HS-3s were completed before the project was cancelled in November 1918.

Technical data – HS-1L	
ENGINE	One 360hp Liberty 12
WINGSPAN	62ft 1in
LENGTH	38ft 6in
HEIGHT	14ft 7in
WING AREA	653sq/ft
EMPTY WEIGHT	4,070lb
MAX TAKE-OFF WEIGHT	5,910lb
MAX SPEED	87mph
CLIMB RATE	1,750ft in 10 mins
ENDURANCE	4.2hrs at full throttle
ARMAMENT	Two 0.303in Lewis machine guns, plus 360lb of bombs or depth charges on underwing racks

The first HS-1 (HS standing for Model H with a single engine), which was initially powered by a 200hp Curtiss V-X-3 driving a three-blade propeller. On October 21, 1917, the same aircraft trialled the 360hp Liberty engine, which was fitted to all production machines.

F-5L

Development

One of several European designs selected for mass production in the US during 1917, the F-5L never carried a Curtiss designation. An evolution of the original America flying-boat of 1914 that was partly designed by Lt Porte, the F-5L came about as the RNAS had commissioned improved versions of the original machine. The British production development of the Model H was the F.2; the 'F' stood for Felixstowe where it was designed.

Design

While the improved hull was designed by Lt Porte, the wings of the F-5, tail unit and power arrangement were pure Curtiss. The design of Porte's F-5 was produced in parallel with the Curtiss H-16 – the main difference being the engines. The British-built F-5s had 345hp Rolls-Royce Eagle engines, while the US-built versions were powered by Liberty engines and, as such, were designated the F-5L. The F-5L and improved Liberty-powered H-16 were very similar aircraft apart from the former's horn-balanced parallel-chord aileron and balanced rudder. The F-5L had different hull lines and an open cockpit rather than the enclosed cabin of the H-16.

Several F-5Ls were converted to civilian use for passenger operations, including a ten-seat version modified by Aeromarine Plane and Motor Co, which redesignated the flying-boat as the Aeromarine 75.

Service

The F-5L entered US Navy service late in World War One but was destined to remain the standard patrol aircraft for a decade until it was replaced by the Naval Aircraft Factory PN-12. The only other military force to fly the F-5L was the Argentine Navy. By 1922, the F-5Ls were redesignated as the PN-5 (P = Patrol and N = Navy) and, the following year, a pair of new F-5L hulls were fitted with new wings and a pair of 525hp Wright T-2 engines; these became PN-7s. Further duplicated models were built with metal hulls and these were designated PN.8.

Aeromarine Airways operated its Aeromarine 75 from 1920 to 1924 on routes between Key West and Havana, and air mail routes from New York City to Atlantic City, and Cleveland to Detroit.

Production

In total, 228 F-5Ls were built: 60 by Curtiss, 30 by Canadian Aeroplanes Ltd; and 138 by the US Naval Aircraft Factory. Post-1918, the price for the F-5L sold direct from the US Navy was $12,400, while a new-build machine ranged from $20,495 to $56,099, minus the engines.

Technical data – F-5L	
ENGINE	Two 400hp Liberty 12A
WINGSPAN	103ft 9¼in
LENGTH	49ft 3¾in
HEIGHT	18ft 9¼in
WING AREA	1,397sq/ft
EMPTY WEIGHT	8,720lb
MAX TAKE-OFF WEIGHT	13,600lb
MAX SPEED	90mph
CEILING	5,500ft
RANGE	830 miles
ARMAMENT	Six to eight 0.3in machine guns on flexible mounts, plus up to 920lb of bombs

The first Curtiss-built F-5L, pictured in July 1927, with a post-war tail modification.

Oriole (Model 17)

Development

Originally known as the Experimental 519 and Design L-72, the Oriole was the first of many Curtiss designs to be marketed under a bird's name rather than a model number. Designed by William Gilmore, the Oriole was an attempt to break into the potentially huge light commercial and sport airplane market, which was expected to expand rapidly straight after World War One. While the market did pick up, it was not fulfilled by new designs but by war-surplus machines such as the JN-4, and Curtiss found itself trying to compete with one of its own products and losing.

Design

The Oriole was a three-seat, general-purpose biplane, with one forward cockpit for the pilot and one larger cockpit for two passengers behind. The passenger's seats were staggered to give extra shoulder room without widening the fuselage. Access was via a small door in the side of the fuselage; a feature that would become standard on all American-built three-seaters into the 1930s. The Oriole was fitted with an electric starter as standard, one of several selling points that did not capture the consumer imagination and was not a common feature on aircraft until many years later. The Oriole was beautifully finished with rounded contours and a laminated plywood skin, while power was provided by a 90hp Curtiss OX-5 in early aircraft and the 150hp K-6 or 160hp C-6 in later machines. The latter C-6 powered aircraft had its wingspan increased from 36ft to 40ft in an effort to improve performance.

Service

The Oriole first appeared in June 1919 and was optimistically presented at a price of $9,850, but the flooded market forced Curtiss to reduce the OX-5 powered machines to $3,000, and $4,800 for C-6 models. Sales were inevitably poor even after the price had been slashed, but some success was achieved during the early 1920s on the racing circuit. One particular machine, the company-owned Oriole, was flown by Curtiss test pilot CS 'Casey' Jones who won several prizes in early post-war races.

Many Orioles were sold in a part-built state to small aircraft manufacturers that were trying to find their feet and were using the basic airframe to complement their own designs. These included the Curtiss-Ireland Comet designed by GS Ireland who married an Oriole to a set of single-bay wings, and the Pitcairn Orowing with short-span wings, tailplane and undercarriage joined to a Pitcairn-designed light fuselage made of steel-tube.

By 1927, all US civilian aircraft were required to be licensed but exactly how many Orioles remained is unclear. None ever received an Approved Type Certificate but a few were licensed for commercial operation following an individual inspection. Only one complete airframe survives today at the Glenn H Curtiss Museum, although a further four airframes are in storage, one with Kermit Weeks and three with Century Aviation.

Production

Exact production numbers of the Oriole are unknown, but it is generally presumed that no more than 50 were built.

Technical data – Oriole (long span)	
ENGINE	One 160hp Curtiss C-6 inline piston engine
WINGSPAN	40ft
LENGTH	36ft 9in
HEIGHT	12ft 4in
WING AREA	900sq ft
EMPTY WEIGHT	5,130lb
MAX TAKE-OFF	7,450lb
MAX SPEED	107mph
RANGE	475 miles
ACCOMMODATION	One pilot, two passengers

A Curtiss Oriole "Racer" with non-standard exhaust and modified rudder.

Eagle I, II and III (Model 19)

Development

Designed by William Gilmore, in anticipation of the demand for new passenger-carrying aircraft, the Eagle was built in limited numbers for a market that was not yet ready. Using the same construction methods and structure as the Oriole, albeit on a larger scale, the Eagle was out-sold on the American market by ex-military machines that had been converted.

Design

The Eagle was a conventional three-bay biplane with equal span, unstaggered wings and a wide-track, double-bogie undercarriage. The latter was enclosed in large, streamlined metal fairings, a feature that was not generally employed until the 1930s. The streamlined fuselage accommodated six to eight passengers in the first aircraft in a high standard of comfort complete with large windows. The crew had its own fully enclosed cockpit – a major departure from the open-cockpit of former military machines.

Built in three versions, the Eagle I was powered by three 150hp K-6 or 160hp C-6 engines while the Eagle II was powered by two 400hp C-12 engines. The Eagle III was a single-engined machine with 400hp Liberty 12 engine. The three aircraft that were built were purchased by the United States Army Air Service (USAAS); two of them were converted into staff transports and one into an ambulance.

Service

The first Eagle I made its maiden flight in August 1919, and all subsequent sales were slow as the expected boom in commercial aviation never happened. On the maiden flight of the sole Eagle II one of the 400hp C-12 engines failed. The aircraft never flew again as a twin-engine aircraft because the combined 800hp of the two engines was too much for the Eagle's airframe.

The Eagle III hit the headlines for all the wrong reasons on May 28, 1921, when the sole ambulance conversion, serialled 64243, crashed during a thunderstorm while trying to land at Morgantown, Maryland. Serving with the 1st Provision Air Brigade at the time, the pilot, 1st Lt Stanley M Ames, and all six passengers onboard were killed.

Production

Approximately 20 aircraft, in total, were constructed, made up of 16 Eagle Is, one Eagle II and three Eagle IIIs.

Technical data – Eagle I, II and III	
ENGINE	(I) Three 150hp Curtiss K-6 or three 160hp C-6; (II) two 400hp C-12; (III) one 400hp Liberty 12
WINGSPAN	(I) 61ft 4in; (II and III) 64ft 4½in
LENGTH	(I) 36ft 9in; (II) 36ft 7in; (III) 37ft 2⁹⁄₁₆in
HEIGHT	(I) 12ft 4in; (II) 12ft 11in; (III) 13ft 6¹⁄₁₆in
WING AREA	(I) 900sq ft; (II and III) 937sq ft
EMPTY WEIGHT	(I) 5,130lb; (II) 5,310lb; (III) 4,245lb
GROSS WEIGHT	(I) 7,450lb; (II) 8,690lb; (III) 7,425lb
MAX SPEED	(I) 107mph; (II) 124mph; (III) 100mph
RANGE	(I) 475 miles; (II) 750 miles
ACCOMMODATION	(I and II) two pilots and six passengers; (III) one pilot and nine passengers

The ill-fated Eagle III air ambulance, 64243, which was lost in a thunderstorm while trying to land at Morgantown, Maryland, on May 28, 1921. Four of six passengers killed were senior United States Air Army Service (USAAS) officers.

Miscellaneous Types

Night Mail to XF13C

During the interwar years, despite the economic slowdown during the Great Depression, Curtiss kept designing and building aircraft, a number of which were also inherited from other aircraft companies. Some examples of the latter were the Standard J-1, the Night Mail of 1922 – a derivative of the J-1, and the Orenco Model D fighter, which was retrospectively given the Curtiss designation Model 26. The US Navy TS-1 carrier fighter was also built by Curtiss and later designated as the Model 28, while the Martin NBS-1 was built by the company and designated as the Model 30. The US Navy Bureau of Aeronautics CS Scout was built by Curtiss as the Model 31 and the Bleeker SX5-1 helicopter of 1929 was built by Curtiss. The same year, Curtiss bought the Moth Aircraft Corporation, which had been building the DH.60 under license; the aircraft was redesignated as the Curtiss-Wright Moth 60GMW. Other requisitions and subsequent renamings included the Reid Rambler, became the Curtiss-Reid Rambler in 1928, as did many Travel Air designs, such as the Model 6000, which became the C-W 6.

Curtiss's own designs of this period were the Seagull (Model 18), effectively a refurbished version of the MF flying-boat; only 16 were sold, customers generally preferring the war surplus machines because they were much cheaper. A further attempt to sell the Seagull produced the Crane (Model 20) in 1924, which featured an amphibious capability, and the Model 25, also called the Seagull.

Another design produced for the US Navy Bureau of Aeronautics was the CT (Model 24), which was an unusual three-seat torpedo-bomber with a monoplane wing with three nacelles attached. The central nacelle was for the crew flanked by two more for the engines, twin floats and booms, which extended to the tail unit. Finally the SX4-1 (Model 34) flying-boat was the last aircraft to be designed by Glenn Curtiss in 1922. Curtiss wanted a sport aircraft to operate from his Florida home, the machine being towed into the air by using a speed boat.

While not achieving any firm orders from the US Army, the XP-31 Swift taught Curtiss a great deal about structural design as the age of the monoplane approached.

At least two designs built for other companies were developed into Curtiss designs, including the NBS-4 (Model 36) night bomber, which evolved from the NBS-1, and the F4C-1 fighter (which exploited the Model TS). The latter was the first Curtiss fighter to serve the US Navy.

In 1925, the Lark (Model 41) appeared; a smaller version of the Carrier Pigeon, the type was commercially unsuccessful and only three were built. One Tanager (Model 54) was built to take part in the Guggenheim Safe Airplane Competition in 1929 but ended up costing Curtiss the $100,000 prize when the company was sued by Handley Page for using its patented leading-edge slots. The Teal (Model 57) was a good-looking monoplane amphibian and appeared in 1930 just as private flying began to slump during the early stages of the depression.

The XP-10 experimental fighter was the company's last design of the 1920s and, with the new decade, the O-40 Raven (Model 62) introduced new structural and aerodynamic concepts. Five Ravens were built, the aircraft featured a metal monocoque fuselage, metal frames and metal-skinned wings. The XP-31 Swift all-metal fighter followed but fared no better than the Raven. The XF13C (Model 70) was a monoplane fighter with retractable undercarriage and was introduced in 1932 at a time when the US Navy was more comfortable with biplanes. Despite presenting the fighter to the US Navy as a biplane, albeit with reduced performance, no orders followed.

A development of the US Navy's TS-1, this single-seat, carrier-based fighter was turned into the F4C-1 by Curtiss, but did not secure any orders.

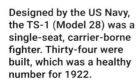

Designed by the US Navy, the TS-1 (Model 28) was a single-seat, carrier-borne fighter. Thirty-four were built, which was a healthy number for 1922.

Curtiss Racers

Model 22 to R3C

Curtiss became involved in racing aircraft when the company was approached by millionaire Mr S Cox in 1920, with a request to build him a pair of machines for the James Gordon Bennett Trophy air race. The two aircraft, named *Texas Wildcat* and *Cactus Kitten*, were the Cox Racers (Model 22), powered by a 427hp C-12 inline engine. Only the Texas Wildcat was tested in time for the race in France but was wrecked in a landing accident. Cactus Kitten returned to the US, was fitted with a set of short-span triplane wings and later came second in the 1921 Pulitzer Trophy Race.

It was another Curtiss racing machine that won the Pulitzer race, in the shape of the Model 23, designated as the CR-1 and CR-2 by the US Navy. Withdrawn by the US Navy, Curtiss "borrowed" the CR-2 and entered the race with test pilot Bert Acosta at the controls. Both CR-1 and CR-2 were biplanes that were powered by the CD-12 inline engine and both were later converted to seaplanes (Model 23A) to compete in the 1923 Schneider Trophy as CR-3s. Re-engined with a 465hp D-12 with Curtiss-Read metal propellers, the two racing seaplanes finished first and second.

Not to be outdone, the US Army decided that it needed a few racing machines and an order was placed for a pair of R-6s, a development of the CR-3. More aerodynamic than their predecessors, aided by wing surface radiators, the two R-6s took first and second place in the 1922 Pulitzer race and the same year, raised the world speed record to 236.587mph. In 1923, the US Navy ordered a pair of R2C-1s (Model 32) from Curtiss with 507hp D-12A engines, which proved to be more than adequate to take first and second in the 1923 Pulitzer race. One R2C-1 also raised the world speed record to 266.59mph before it was sold to the US Army for $1 and redesignated as an R-8. The other R2C-1 was converted to R2C-2 (Model 32A) and served as a trainer for the 1925 Schneider competition.

The US Amy and Navy worked together in 1925 and ordered three new racing aircraft, the R3C-1 (Model 42) with V-1400 engines. Two of them were entered in the 1925 Pulitzer race, the US Army

The CR-1 (Model 23) along with the CR-2, was converted to a seaplane configuration to compete in the 1923 Schneider Trophy race as CR-3s.

coming first and the US Navy second. Fitted with floats and redesignated as the R3C-2 (Model 42A), all three were entered into the 1925 Schneider Trophy. The US Navy subsequently withdrew and the race was won by Lt James H Doolittle in R3C-2 A6979. The US only had to win the Schneider Trophy one more time to secure it, and for the 1926 race, only enough funds were available to re-engine the R3C-2 with a 700hp Packard 2A-1500 engine to become the R3C-3. With a potential average speed of 255mph, the US prepared for another victory but the R3C-3 crashed during trials. A second R3C-2 was refurbished and fitted with a 708hp Curtiss V-1550 engine but was forced to retire during the race, leaving the third standard R3C-2 to take second place behind the Italian Macchi M.39.

Technical data – R3C-2	
ENGINE	One 565hp Curtiss V-1400
WINGSPAN	22ft
LENGTH	22ft
HEIGHT	10ft 4in
WING AREA	144sq ft
EMPTY WEIGHT	2,135lb
MAX TAKE-OFF	2,738lb
MAX SPEED	245mph
RANGE	290 miles at full power

Lt James "Jimmy" H Doolittle with his R3C-2, A6979, after winning the 1925 Schneider Trophy race at Baltimore, at an average speed of 232mph.

The winner of the 1922 Pulitzer air race was 1st Lt Russell Maughan, in the second R-6 to be built and at an average speed of 205.856mph, which broke the closed-course record up to 200km.

PW-8 (Model 33/34)

Development
Drawing on its experience of designing and building the Curtiss racing biplanes, the company designed a fighter that would mark the beginning of the highly successful Hawk family and would continue on into the late 1930s.

Design
The PW-8 was a two-bay biplane with heavily staggered wings and a sleek aerodynamic fuselage, helped by the slender cross-section of the D-12 inline piston engine. Of traditional construction, the PW-8 did see a change in practise with the introduction of a wire-braced, welded steel-tube fuselage and a split-axle undercarriage. An additional aerodynamic feature was the use of wing surface radiators, another legacy of the Curtiss racing biplanes, although this system would be replaced by a more traditional radiator. The wings were made of wood, while the tail surfaces were made up of an aluminium framework.

Service
The prototype PW-8 (Model 33) made its maiden flight in January 1923 and, on April 27, at a cost of $16,000, was purchased by the US Army. The first of three prototypes later redesignated as XPW-8, the second machine was a refined version of the first. The third, XPW-8A, had new wings fitted and a core-type radiator.

A production order for 25 PW-8s was placed by the US Army on September 25, 1923, the first of which arrived at the 17th Pursuit Group (PG) in June 1924 in a process that would last for 12 months. On June 23, 1924, 1st Lt RL Maughan in PW-8 24-204 carried out the first dawn-to-dusk crossing of the US. Five refuelling stops were made over a distance of 2,670 miles. The flight, although carried out by a US Army aircraft, was substantially assisted by Curtiss, which was part of the deal that had been agreed for the 25-strong production order.

Lt Moffatt standing in front of his PW-8 in which he set a new record flight on March 9, 1924, when he flew from Boston to New York and back in 2hrs 15mins.

The XPW-8A (Model 34) was delivered to the US Army on September 4, 1924, and the following month achieved third place in the annual Pulitzer Trophy Race. The aircraft was then returned to the factory and had a set of tapered wings fitted and was redesignated as the XPW-8B. It was this aircraft that was the first building block of the later P-1 Hawk fighter.

XPW-8 No.1 was modified into a two-seater by US Army engineers in 1923 and was designated as the Corps Observation Experimental (CO-X). The aircraft was entered into the 1923 Liberty Engine Builders Trophy race, which was specifically designed for military two-seaters. Objections were raised and the CO-X was forced to withdraw from the competition presumably because it was a modification, and a hasty one at that, rather than a pure design.

Production

Three PW-8s (later designated XPW-8 by the Army) serialled 23-1201–03 (including one XPW-8 No.1 [later temporarily converted to the two-seat CO-C], one No 2 [prototype of production aircraft] and one XPW-8A later converted to XPW-8B); and 25 production PW-8s, serialled 24-201–25 were built.

Technical data – PW-8	
ENGINE	One 440hp Curtiss D-12
WINGSPAN	32ft
LENGTH	23ft 1in
EMPTY WEIGHT	2,185lb
LOADED WEIGHT	3,155lb
MAX SPEED	171mph at sea level
INITIAL CLIMB RATE	1,830 ft/min
SERVICE CEILING	20,350ft
RANGE	544 miles
ARMAMENT	Two fixed fuselage-mounted 0.3in machine-guns

The XPW-8B, which featured a tunnel-type radiator under the forward fuselage; a key feature of all subsequent production Hawks and Falcons.

Carrier Pigeon (Model 40)

Development
The Carrier Pigeon was the Curtiss entry into the 1925 US Post Office competition for a new, single-seat mailplane to replace the reliable but ageing Airco DH.4. It was one of America's first, if not the world's first, aircraft designed specifically for the US Airmail service rather than being a conversion of a war surplus machine.

Design
The Carrier Pigeon was designed to a set of very simple postal specifications that called for strength, reliability and easy maintenance. The aircraft also needed to be capable of carrying out a night flight from Chicago to New York in one stop and be fitted with the reliable and powerful Liberty 12 engine.

The aircraft's wings had wooden frames and used the thick Aerofoil USA-27, while the fuselage was made of steel-tube and the frame of the tail was aluminium. One unusual feature of the aircraft was its interchangeable upper and lower wings. There was no centre section and the lower wing was separated by the fuselage and was of greater span than the upper wing. Even the ailerons, rudder, elevators, fin and tailplane were interchangeable. A sturdy wide-track undercarriage with independent main gear units helped the Carrier Pigeon to operate from ill-prepared fields. The aircraft had watertight mail holds fore and aft of the pilot's open cockpit with a capacity for 40,000 airmail letters up to a weight of 1,000lb.

A larger, modernized version known as the Carrier Pigeon II was built in 1929 with a 600hp geared water-cooled Conqueror engine driving a three-blade propeller. The Mk II had wooden-framed wings, box spars, aluminium tail surfaces and an aluminium fuselage. The main fuel tank could hold 175 gallons.

Service
The first of ten Carrier Pigeons was entered into the 1,900 miles-long 1925 Edsel B Ford Reliability Tour and, in the hands of Charles S Jones, the aircraft finished seventh out of 17 starters to win a $350 prize. All ten Carrier Pigeon Is served with the National Air Transport Inc; the first service was flown on May 12, 1926, between Chicago, Illinois and Dallas. The aircraft flew 776,351 miles without incident during the type's first year of service and only one crash was recorded during the Carrier Pigeon's entire career, which came to an end on February 9, 1934. The sole loss was the prototype, serialled with US Post Office Fleet No.602, which struck trees near Montpelier, killing the pilot, Arthur R Smith.

Production
Ten Carrier Pigeon Is (serialled K-5015-1–11) and three Carrier Pigeon IIs registered as 958A, 311N and 369N (serialled G-1–G-3) were built.

Technical data – Carrier Pigeon I and II	
ENGINE	(I) One 400hp Liberty 12; (II) one 600hp Curtiss G1V-1570 Conqueror
WINGSPAN	(I) 41ft 11in; (II) 47ft 5⅜in
LENGTH	(I) 28ft 9½in; (II) 34ft 6¼in
HEIGHT	(I) 12ft 1in; (II) 13ft 5in
WING AREA	(I) 505sq ft; (II) 550sq ft
EMPTY WEIGHT	(I) 3,603lb; (II) 4,235lb
GROSS WEIGHT	(I) 5,620lb; (II) 7,600lb
MAX SPEED	(I) 125mph; (II) 150mph
SERVICE CEILING	(I) 12,800ft; (II) 14,200ft
MAX RANGE	(I) 525 miles; (II) 650 miles

The Carrier Pigeon II was virtually a new aircraft; its only resemblance to the original was that it was a single-seat mail and cargo carrier.

F6C Hawk (Model 34)

Development
Virtually identical to the US Army's P-1 Hawk, the US Navy placed an order for nine F6C-1 Hawk fighters in 1925. Intended to serve the USMC as land-based fighters, larger orders followed, and the type went on to serve from two US aircraft carriers during the late 1920s.

Design
The initial order of nine F6C-1s was changed to five, with the four remaining Hawks delivered as F6C-2s complete with arrestor gear, strengthened fuselages and high-impact undercarriages so that they could handle carrier operations. By 1927, the US Navy had decided that the type would be suited to carrier operations and placed an order for a modified version of the F6C-2, the F6C-3 (Model 34E). A follow up order for 31 F6C-4s followed after the first F6C-1 (redesignated the XF6C-4) had been trialled with a 420hp Pratt & Whitney R-1340 Wasp radial engine rather than the earlier model's Curtiss D-12 water-cooled inline engines. Both the F6C-1 and -2 could be fitted with twin floats, although only the F6C-3 used them operationally.

Service
The five F6C-1s entered service with VF-9M, USMC, and were later joined by the rotary-powered XF6C-4 for operations from airfields from 1926. The four F6C-2s joined VF-2, US Navy, aboard the USS *Langley*, the US's only aircraft carrier, up to 1927. All 35 F6C-3s were ordered in 1927 and joined VF-5S (redesignated VF-1B), US Navy, and VF-8M, USMC, aboard the USS *Lexington,* which was commissioned on December 14, 1927. All 31 F6C-4s joined VF-2B, US Navy, on USS *Langley* until the type was withdrawn in 1930, the water-cooled earlier models having already been withdrawn from carrier operations by 1928.

   One F6C-1, A7128, was part of a strong US and Curtiss-dominated field that competed in the 1926 Schneider Trophy race. Lt William Tomlinson, in the D-12-A-powered Hawk, finished in fourth place (only four aircraft remained in the race). An F6C-3, A7144, was transformed into a high-wing racing monoplane complete with an internal radiator and low-drag undercarriage in 1929. Redesignated as the F6C-6, it finished fourth in a "free-for-all" race. Another F6C-3, A7147, won the 1930 Curtiss Marine Trophy but was later dramatically modified into the XF6C-6. Installed with a 770hp V-1570 Conqueror engine, the aircraft was converted into a monoplane for the 1930 Thompson Trophy Race. Unfortunately, it crashed during the race.

Production
In total, 75 F6C Hawks were built, comprising five F6C-1s (Model 34C); four F6C-2s (Model 34D); 35 F6C-3s (Model 34E) and 31 F6C-4s (Model 34H) at $11,808 each, delivered between 1925 and 1928.

Technical data – F6C-4 Hawk	
ENGINE	One 410hp Pratt & Whitney R-1340 Wasp
WINGSPAN	37ft 6in
LENGTH	22ft 6in
HEIGHT	10ft 11in
WING AREA	252sq ft
EMPTY WEIGHT	1,980lb
MAX TAKE-OFF	3,171lb
MAX SPEED	155mph at sea level
SERVICE CEILING	22,900ft
RANGE	340 miles
ARMAMENT	Two fuselage-mounted, forward-firing synchronized 0.3in machine-guns plus light bombs on underwing racks

The US Navy Schneider Cup Team in front of an F6C-1 Hawk on August 19, 1926. Lt William G Tomlinson is second from left; he was later promoted to rear admiral.

P-1 and P-6 Hawk (Model 34/35)

Development

Following successful flight testing of the XPW-8B, with new tapered wings and several other modifications, an order of 15 production aircraft was requested by the US Army. This latest fighter was designated the P-1, the P standing for "Pursuit," which would remain the standard method of defining fighters until it was replaced by "F" in the late 1940s.

Design

The P-1 Hawk (Model 34A) was effectively a production version of the XPW-8 while the P-1A (Model 34G) introduced a new wing and a redesigned tailplane along with several other improvements. The P-1B (Model 34I) was improved again with a 435hp Curtiss V1150-3 engine, larger diameter wheels and a rounded radiator. The P-1C (Model 34O) had better brakes and various equipment changes that raised its gross weight. The P-2 to P-5 aircraft were all used for test work and were fitted with a variety of engines including the Curtiss V-1400, R-1454 and the Pratt & Whitney Wasp, all with and without turbo-superchargers.

The P-6 Hawk was the successful end result of combining a 600hp V-1570 engine with a P-1C airframe, which was redesignated as the XP-6 (Model 34P) followed by a second machine, the XP-6A (Model 34K), without tapered wings and wing surface radiators. The US Army ordered 18 improved XP-6s with Prestone-cooled V-1570 engines as an evaluation batch, followed by another 18, designated P-6A, half of which were fitted with Prestone-cooled V-1570-23 engines. One XP-6B was built and an order for the P-6C was redesignated and cancelled in favour of the P-6E. The P-6Ds were P-6As, which had been re-engined with the V-1570-C Conqueror engine.

The P-6E was by far the best of the breed to serve with the USAAC, and its manoeuvrability alone made it an instant hit with pursuit squadrons. It had a slimmer fuselage with its radiator mounted forward of the undercarriage, the latter comprising single struts and main wheels shrouded in spats.

Several trainer variants were also produced, known as the AT-4 and AT-5. Overstressed and under-powered, the trainers were not a success and, after being fitted with D-12 engines, were redesignated as the P-1D, E and F.

Service

The first P-1 Hawk was delivered to the US Army on August 17, 1925. Ten of them initially served with the 27th and 94th Pursuit Squadron, 1st Pursuit Group, at Selfridge Field, Michigan. The P-1A also joined 17, 27 and 94 Squadrons by late 1925. Numbers had increased by 1928 and the few AT-4 and AT-5 trainers that had been built were allocated to the 43rd Pursuit Squadron (School) at Kelly Field but, by 1930, the P-1 Hawk was already being withdrawn from operational service.

Deliveries of the P-6E began in 1931 in order to serve with the 17th and 94th Pursuit Squadrons and the 33rd Pursuit Squadron, 8th Pursuit Group at Langley Field, Virginia. The P-6E attrition rate was high, although at least one remained in USAAF service until 1942, even though the type was withdrawn as an operational fighter in 1937.

Production

The P-1 to P-6 Hawk family was built between 1925 and 1932, the main production variants were the P-1 (10), P-1A (25), P-1B (25), P-1C (33), P-1D (24 AT-4 conversions), P-1E (four AT-5 conversions), P-1F (24 AT-5A conversions), P-2 (five), P-3A (five), P-5 (four), AT-4 (40, of which 35 were converted to P-1Ds and five as AT-5), AT-5 (five, later converted to P-1Es), AT-5A (31, later converted to P-1Fs), P-6A (18), P-6D (seven), P-6E (46) and P-6S Hawk I (three to Cuba, one to Japan).

Technical data – P-6E Hawk	
ENGINE	One 700hp Curtiss V-1750C Conqueror
WINGSPAN	31ft 6in
LENGTH	23ft 2in
HEIGHT	8ft 11in
WING AREA	252sq/ft
EMPTY WEIGHT	2,669lb
MAX-TAKEOFF WEIGHT	3,436lb
MAX SPEED	198mph
SERVICE CEILING	24,700ft
RANGE	285 miles
ARMAMENT	Two fuselage-mounted, forward-firing synchronized 0.3in machine-guns

The sole XP-6A (Model 34Q), 26-295, was modified as a racing aircraft for the 1927 National Air Races. Fitted with a boosted Conqueror engine, the aircraft won the unlimited race at an average speed of 201mph.

Curtiss P-1E, 27-238, pictured at Kelly Field whilst serving with the 43rd Pursuit Squadron (School) at Kelly Field. This aircraft was originally built as an AT-5 trainer before conversion to P-1E.

F7C-1 Seahawk (Model 43)

Development

Drawing heavily from the design of the Hawk and Falcon, the Seahawk was a private venture that endeavored to meet a new US Navy requirement for a radial-engined, single-seat carrier-based fighter. Designed exclusively for the US Navy for the first time, rather than a conversion of a US Army type, the Seahawk, despite being built in low numbers, served the USMC for five years.

Design

The Curtiss Model 43 was powered by the same engine as the F6C-4, the 450hp R-1340B Wasp radial, and also featured the same three-piece upper mainplane sweepback of the Falcon. A new design feature of the Model 43 was the installation of the main fuel tanks on each side of the forward fuselage. Mounted outside of the structure, the tanks were contoured into the aircraft to form part of the streamlining. This same design feature was also later incorporated into the F8C-2 Helldiver.

While the prototype, the XF7C-1, could be operated as a land or seaplane, the production machines, F7C-1 Seahawks, were solely designed as landplanes. Production aircraft also had a longer wingspan and no propeller spinners. One was converted to an XF7C-3 to evaluate the 575hp Wright R-1820-1 and demonstrate full-span flaps. One XF7C-3 demonstrator was also built for China with four 0.3in machine-guns, modified interplane struts and ailerons on all four mainplanes. Another production F7C-1, A7655, was employed for experimental trials including the testing of a "biplane" propeller.

Service

The XF7C-1, an unofficial US Navy designation, was first flown on February 28, 1927. The aircraft was known to the company as the Curtiss Navy Fighter. After placing a production order for 16 F7C-1s (serialled A7654–A7670), the prototype was purchased by the US Navy, redesignated as an F7C-1 and given the proceeding serial (A7653) to those applied to the production aircraft. All 16 production aircraft and later, the prototype, served with VF-5M, USMC, based at Quantico, Virginia, and later with VF-9M in 1930 as part of an air display team named "The Red Devils." The F7C-1 Seahawk remained in USMC service until 1933, and today one surviving example, A7667, is on display in the National Museum of Naval Aviation, Pensacola, Florida.

Production

One XF7C-1 prototype was built at a cost of $82,450, plus 16 production F7C-1s for the USMC at a cost of $17,111 each, delivered between August 1927 and 1929.

Technical data – F7C-1 Seahawk	
ENGINE	One 450hp Pratt & Whitney R-1340B Wasp
WINGSPAN	32ft 8in
LENGTH	22ft ⅞in
HEIGHT	9ft 8½in
WING AREA	275sq/ft
EMPTY WEIGHT	2,053lb
MAX-TAKEOFF WEIGHT	2,782lb
MAX SPEED	155mph at sea level
SERVICE CEILING	22,100ft
RANGE	355 miles
ARMAMENT	Two fuselage-mounted, forward-firing synchronized 0.3in machine-guns

The prototype Model 43, designated as the XF7C-1 by the US Navy and the Curtiss Navy Fighter (written on the tail) by the company. Purchased by the US Navy, the aircraft served alongside the production machines as F7C-1 Seahawk A7653.

N2C and Fledgling (Model 48/51)

Development

By late 1927, the US Navy was on the hunt for a new primary trainer and, as a result, Curtiss presented the Fledgling, an aircraft that followed virtually the same design philosophy as the JN-4. A demand for civilian trainers and the expansion of the Curtiss Flying Service raised some interest in the type, which was ultimately crushed by the onset of the Great Depression.

Design

The trainer featured a two-bay, equal span biplane with the instructor and pupil in open tandem cockpits. The variety produced for the 1928 Navy was designated XN2C-1 (Model 48). Power was provided by a 220hp Wright J-5, and the aircraft could be operated as a land or floatplane. The production order that followed was designated N2C-1, retaining the J-5 engine, while the next production run, designated N2C-2 (Model 48A), featured a 240hp Wright J-6-7, higher gross weight, greater ceiling and an improved maximum speed.

The commercial version was known as the Fledgling (Model 51) with power provided by a 170hp Curtiss Challenger engine. A Fledgling Junior, with a reduced wingspan, was also produced but was not successful. A handful of Fledgling J-1s with the Wright J-6-5 and the Fledgling J-2 with the Wright J-6-7 were also built.

Service

The three XN2C-1 prototypes (A7650 to A7652) were purchased by the US Navy in 1928 and, before the year was over, they were joined by the first of 31 production N2C-1s (A8020–A8050). Painted in bright orange and yellow, each aircraft cost $6,550 minus government-furnished equipment (GFE). The N2C-2 quickly followed into service, a few examples of which survived into the late 1930s after conversion to pilotless radio control drones (redesignated as A-3 by the USAAF) with a tricycle undercarriage.

All of the 109 civilian Fledglings that were built were used by the Curtiss Flying Service and were finished with yellow wings and tailplane and an orange fuselage. Several aircraft were operated in small numbers or trialled including the Brazilian, Colombian, Czechoslovakian, Iranian* and Turkish Air Forces.

Production

Approximately 160 N2Cs were built, made up of three XN2C-1s (Model 48), 31 N2C-1s, and 20 N2C-2s (Model 48A). At least seven N2C-1 kits were supplied to the Turkish Air Force in 1933. In total, there were 109 (Model 51) Fledgling aircraft, four converted to J-1 and two to J-2.

---

* One N2C-1 is believed to have been gifted to the Iranians by Turkey.

Technical data – N2C-1	
ENGINE	One 220hp Wright J-5
WINGSPAN	39ft 2in
LENGTH	27ft 4in
HEIGHT	10ft 4in
WING AREA	365sq/ft
EMPTY WEIGHT	2,135lb
MAX-TAKEOFF WEIGHT	2,832lb
MAX SPEED	109mph
SERVICE CEILING	15,100ft
RANGE	366 miles

A production N2C-1, A8048: one of a second batch of 31 aircraft ordered by the US Navy in 1928 at a cost of $6,500 minus equipment.

O-1/F8C Falcon (Model 37/38/44) Development

The first two-seat Falcon appeared in 1923 as the Curtiss entry in an Air Service fly-off competition for a new observation machine, powered by a Liberty engine. The Falcons have all but been erased from pre-war aviation history simply because they were not as glamorous as the Hawk fighters, despite nearly as many Falcons being built as Hawks for the US Army and US Navy. The US Army went on to operate 11 different designations with six different engines and the US Navy operated two variants with two engines. The most significant are covered here.

Design

The first Falcon was designated as the L-113 (Model 37) but was evaluated as the XO-1 in 1924. A conventional unequal-span biplane powered by a 510hp Packard 1A-500, the wings were made from wood and the fuselage was built up with aluminium tubing and braced with steel tie rods. The production machine was the O-1 (Model 37A); ten were ordered, nine with D-12 engines and the tenth with a Liberty. The O-1B (Model 37B) was the first major production variant and featured refined brakes and a droppable under-fuselage 56-gallon fuel tank. A version for the National Guard was produced as the O-11 (Model 37C) which, apart from a Liberty engine, was similar to the O-1B. The O-1E (Model 37I) followed with a V-1150E engine and further refinements. The O-1G was the final significant production version of the Model 37s with a re-designed pilot's instrument panel and improved gunner's seat.

The O-39 (Model 38A) was powered by a V-1570-25 Conqueror and the engine cowling and radiator were similar to those that were installed in the P-6E Hawk. The A-3 (Model 44) was an attack variant converted from the O-1B with armament increased to two 0.30in machine guns in the lower wing and with provision for 200lb of bombs in underwing racks. The A-3B (Model 37H) followed, which used the same airframe as the O-1E. The US Navy operated the Falcon as the F8C-1 and F8C-3 (Model 37D) in the fighter and light bomber role. All of the US Navy aircraft were redesignated for the observation role to OC-1 and OC-2.

Service

The O-1 Falcon and its wide range of descendants entered USAAC service in 1926 and were destined to remain in service until the mid-1930s. They were not completely retired from the National Guard until October 1937. The Falcon achieved some success commercially with 20 aircraft sold including several mailplane variants and a "Lindbergh Special" demonstrator sold to Charles Lindbergh. In US Navy and USMC service, the type remained until 1935 and sales to overseas customers included the Colombian Air Force where the aircraft saw action in the Colombia–Peru War in 1932–34.

Production

The main production variants of the Falcon were the O-1 (10), O-1B (45, of which 15 were sold to Colombia), O-1C (4), O-1E (41 [at least ten O-1Es were built in Chile; later sold to Brazil]), O-1G (30), O-11 (66), O-39 (10), A-3 (66), A-3B (78), F8C-1 (4), F8C-3 (21), Cyclone Falcons (100) for Colombia and civilian Falcons (20).

Technical data – O-1E Falcon	
ENGINE	One 435hp Curtiss V-1150E
WINGSPAN	38ft
LENGTH	27ft 2in
HEIGHT	10ft 6in
WING AREA	353sq/ft
EMPTY WEIGHT	2,922lb
MAX-TAKEOFF WEIGHT	4,347lb
MAX SPEED	141mph
SERVICE CEILING	15,300ft
RANGE	630 miles
ARMAMENT	One fixed synchronized forward-firing 0.30in Browning machine gun and twin 0.30in Lewis machine gun on a Scarff mounting

Right: Using the same airframe as the O-1E observation aircraft, 78 A-3Bs (Model 37H) were built. This aircraft, 30-25, belongs to the 13th Attack Squadron, 3rd Attack Group, and is pictured on May 16, 1933.

Below: The first major production Falcon was the O-1B, of which 45 were ordered in 1927. This aircraft, 27-263, had been converted to the sole XO-18 with a 610hp Curtiss H-1640-1 Chieftain engine.

B-2 Condor (Model 52) and Condor 18 (Model 53)

Development

There was heavy competition for production contracts for military aircraft by the mid-1920s and, even if successful, and bids were made, orders were rarely high. The USAAC needed a new heavy bomber and designs from Keystone, Sikorsky, Fokker and Curtiss were all submitted, the latter presenting the strongest contender with the B-2 Condor (Model 52). However, a design that had not been submitted, the Keystone XLB-6, was also favoured by the USAAC, this aircraft was destined to be ordered in slightly higher numbers and would serve alongside the B-2.

Design

The B-2 Condor descended from the experimental XNBS-4 (Model 36); the bomber inherited the same extended engine nacelles that contained a gunner's cockpit in the rear of each of them. The out-of-date biplane tail unit was also copied from the Model 36, while the general construction of the aircraft was more cutting edge, having welded steel tube truss wing spars and riveted duralumin ribs.

A civilian version of the B-2 was called the Condor 18 (Model 53), which had a redesigned and lengthened fuselage for 18 passengers and an enclosed cockpit for two pilots. The wings were virtually the same as the B-2's for the first three that were built while the remaining three had a dihedral on both upper and lower mainplanes.

Service

The prototype XB-2 Condor was ordered in 1926 and was built at Garden City. Delivered in July 1927, the aircraft was lost on December 1927 with only 59 flying hours on its clock. Despite this setback, the USAAC ordered a dozen B-2 Condors, the first of which was delivered in June 1929. These production aircraft differed from the prototype by having shorter, wider radiators and three-blade propellers. The B-2s joined the USAAC's only heavy bomber unit, the 11th Bomb Squadron, 7th Bombardment Group at Rockwell Field, California, in 1928 but had been withdrawn by 1931. One B-2, fitted with dual controls, was used for experimental flying until 1934. The last B-2 was retired in July 1936, after building a healthy 1889 flying hours.

The Condor 18 first flew in June 1929, by which time the civilian airliner market that the aircraft was pitched at had already been bagged by Ford and Fokker tri-motor machines. All six produced were eventually sold to Eastern Air Transport (EAT) for a price not much above cost in 1931. EAT flew them until the mid-1930s.

Production

Thirteen B-2 Condors (Model 52) were built between 1927 and 1929, comprising one XB-2 (26-211) prototype and 12 production (two ordered in 1928 and ten in 1929) B-2s serialled 28-398, 28-399 and 29-28 to 29-37. Six Condor 18s (Model 53) were registered as NC185H, 725K, 984H (changed to 985V) and 726K to 728K.

Technical data – B-2 Condor and Condor 18	
ENGINE	(B-2) Two 600hp Curtiss GV-1570; (18) two 625hp GV-1570
WINGSPAN	(B-2) 90ft; (18) 91ft 8in
LENGTH	(B-2) 47ft 4½in; (18) 57ft 6in
HEIGHT	16ft 3in
WING AREA	(B-2) 1,496 sq/ft; (18) 1,510 sq/ft
EMPTY WEIGHT	(B-2) 9,300lb; (18) 12,426lb
MAX-TAKEOFF WEIGHT	(B-2) 16,591lb
GROSS WEIGHT	(18) 17,900lb
MAX SPEED	(B-2) 132mph; (18) 145.2mph
SERVICE CEILING	(B-2) 17,100ft; (18) 17,000ft
RANGE	(B-2) 805 miles
ARMAMENT	(B-2) Six 0.30in machine guns, plus a maximum bomb load of 2,508lb

Above: The backbone of the USAAC heavy bomber capability, the B-2 Condor, served from June 1929 until 1931 but a few examples lingered on until the mid-1930s.

Right: The XB-2 Condor prototype, serialled 26-211, which was ordered by the US Army in 1926 and delivered in July 1927. The aircraft was wrecked in December 1927 after only 59 flying hours.

B-2 Condors of the 11th Bomb Squadron (BS), 7th Bomb Group (BG) in formation over Atlantic City, after completing a cross-country flight from their home base at Rockwell Field, California.

Robin (Model 50)

Development
The Robin family of three-seat cabin monoplanes was a huge success story for Curtiss from the late 1920s through to the early 1930s. The Robin did well in the growing US private aircraft market especially when it was sold with a Curtiss OX-5 engine, which kept the price to $4,000. The OX-5 engine cost $250 leading to suggestions that Curtiss designed the Robin to use up its massive stock of the old engine; whether this was true or not, the aircraft certainly went a long way to achieving just that.

Design
Designed for a pilot and two passengers, the Robin was a purposeful, uncomplicated design made of mixed construction. The wings were wood and the fuselage made of steel tubing and with the pilot sat forward at the controls, the cabin was very roomy for a pair of passengers sat side-by-side behind. Early aircraft used the war-surplus OX-5 but many other engines were used such as the 150 and 180hp Wright, the 170 and 185hp Challenger, 165hp Whirlwind and the 110hp Scarab.

   A feature of early Robins was a pair of large flat strut fairings, which were designed to give the aircraft extra lift but quickly proved to be more of a hindrance than a help. Bungee-chord shock absorbers also distinguished the early machines, but these were later replaced by oleo-pneumatic versions. Several Robins were also converted into twin-float seaplanes.

Service
The first of the 769 Robins built took its maiden flight on August 7, 1928. Three more prototypes followed, and it was not long before the orders began to flood in, especially with such a tempting price tag. By mid-1929, peak production was reached when 17 aircraft left the factory each week, making the Robin family the most popular private touring aircraft in the US at the time.

Robin *St Louis* being flown by Dale Jackson and Forest O'Brine is refuelled during the first world refuelling endurance record in July 1929. The aircraft landed after 17 days, 12 hrs, 17mins.

Robins were used to break the world refuelling endurance record on three separate occasions between July 1929 and July 1935. The latter, carried out between June 4 and July 1, saw the aircraft remain aloft for 653hrs 34mins. The Robin was well publicized when Douglas Corrigan announced that he was going to fly his J-1 from New York to Los Angeles on July 17, 1938. The following day, the young Irish-American pilot landed his aircraft in Ireland, an unauthorized transatlantic flight, which he had been previously denied. He claimed it to be a navigational error right up to his death in 2010 and was nicknamed "Wrong Way" Corrigan for his action.

At least seven Robins survive today in museums and in private hands across the US, and two of them are airworthy.

Production

In total, 769 Robins were built, including the Challenger Robin; Robin B (325); Robin B-2; Robin C (50); Robin C-1 (200); Robin C-2 (six); Robin 4C (one); Robin 4C-1 (three); Robin 4C-1A (11); Robin CR; Robin J-1 (+/-40); Robin J-2 (two); Robin M (seven) and the Robin W (small number); and one Robin W was sold to the US Army as a pilotless drone, designated XC-10.

Technical data – Robin C-1	
ENGINE	One 185hp Curtiss Challenger
WINGSPAN	41ft
LENGTH	25ft 1in
HEIGHT	8ft
WING AREA	223 sq/ft
EMPTY WEIGHT	1,700lb
MAX TAKE-OFF WEIGHT	2,600lb
MAX SPEED	120mph
CRUISING SPEED	102mph
SERVICE CEILING	12,700ft
MAX RANGE	300 miles
ACCOMMODATION	One pilot, two passengers (Robin 4C-1A could carry four passengers)

Robin *Lady Rolph* flown by Bobby Trout and Edna Mae Cooper in January 1931 to capture the female endurance record, which they set at five days 2hrs 50mins.

O2C-1 Helldiver (Model 49)

Development

The main production success for Curtiss during the late 1920s was a two-seat fighter-bomber, christened with the intimidating name Helldiver. The aircraft originated with a fighter designation, which incorrectly gave the impression that it was a variant of the F8C-1 Falcon when, in fact, it was a new design. The Helldiver was destined to become the US Navy's first purpose-built dive bomber, although many would serve, more successfully, in the observation role.

Design

Although the Helldiver's roots were firmly entrenched in the early Falcon family, the aircraft differed in many ways. The fuselage structure was welded steel-tube, the wings were made of wood and the tail surfaces were aluminium framed. Internally, the Helldiver featured main fuel tanks, which were built into the sides of the fuselage in front of the cockpit. The forward armament was repositioned from the lower to the upper mainplane; the latter having a reduced area and span. Power was provided by the same Wasp radial installed in the F8C-1/OC-1 Falcon and F6C-4 Hawk. Capable of carrying a single 500lb bomb, the device was carried on a rack that swung clear of the lower fuselage and propeller arc before release.

Service

The first of three XF8C prototypes made its maiden flight in November 1928, only to be lost on December 3 during a test dive. In total, 25 production F8C-4s were ordered by the US Navy and the first machines joined VF-1B on board USS *Saratoga* in 1930. The USMC took delivery of 63 F8C-5s in 1931 and, despite having a fighter designation, the type was used by land-based units for observation

Curtiss F8C-4 Helldiver of VF-1B, USS *Saratoga* circa 1930. Only 25 examples of the F8C-4 were built, at cost of $15,450 each.

duties and was subsequently redesignated as the O2C-1. A further 30 O2C-1s were ordered by the USMC with the majority were serving with reserve units by 1934.

The Helldiver proved to be more useful to the US Navy and USMC as a public-relations aircraft because its performance was unimpressive. However, it was still a tough, reliable machine. It featured in several period films, including *King Kong* and even in the 21st century remake, the type featured again in the final infamous scenes around the Empire State Building.

Production

Two Helldiver prototypes, one XF8C-2 (Model 49) and one XF8C-4 (Model 49A) were followed by 25 production F8C-4s (Model 49Bs) serialled A8421–8445, 63 F8C-5s (re-designated O2C-1) serialled A8446–8456, A8589–8597 and A8748–8790, and later 30 additional O2C-1s serialled A8941–9870.

Technical data – O2C-1 (F8C-5)	
ENGINE	One 450hp Pratt & Whitney R-1340-4 Wasp
WINGSPAN	32ft
LENGTH	25ft 8in
HEIGHT	10ft 3in
WING AREA	308 sq/ft
EMPTY WEIGHT	2,520lb
MAX TAKE-OFF WEIGHT	4,020lb
MAX SPEED	146mph at sea level
SERVICE CEILING	16,250ft
MAX RANGE	720 miles
ARMAMENT	Two fixed and one or two flexibly mounted 0.3in machine-guns and one 500lb or two 116lb underwing bombs

One of the 63 F8C-5s built, which were later re-designated as O2C-1s to reflect their primary role as a land-based observation aircraft.

Kingbird (Model 55)

Development

The Kingbird (Model 55) and Thrush (Model 56) were developed simultaneously, the former being powered by two engines and the latter by one. Unfortunately, by the time a fully functioning production aircraft was available, the Great Depression had gripped the US and only limited orders were forthcoming.

Design

A scaled up, twin-engined version of the Thrush, the Kingbird had increased passenger and baggage capacity and larger fuel tanks. The general layout of the Kingbird was a twin-engine, high-wing strut, braced monoplane of mixed construction. The aircraft had a wide-track undercarriage and a twin-fin and rudder tail unit. The two engines were positioned as close together as possible with the propeller blades only inches apart in front of the nose. This configuration, which attempted to get the engines as close to the centreline as possible, would make the handling of the aircraft much easier if one engine should fail.

Service

Designed by Theodore Paul Wright and Al Wedburg, the prototype, Kingbird C, first flew in May 1929 followed by two Whirlwind-powered prototypes called the Kingbird D-1. The latter was refined into the only production version, the seven-seater Kingbird D-2. 14 D-2s were sold at a cost of $25,555 each to Eastern Air Transport in 1930, and were the only Kingbird sales to a civilian customer. The only other customer for a Kingbird was the US Navy, which ordered a single D-2 for the use of the USMC under the designation RC-1. Delivered in March 1931, the RC-1 serialled 8846 was retired in 1936.

Four other Kingbird variants were produced, the first was the D-3, powered by 330hp Whirlwind engines with reduced passenger capacity but space for 259lb of baggage or mail, plus toilet facilities.

The Kingbird C was converted into the J-1 with 250hp Wright engines but crashed on July 23, 1930. The third prototype was converted into the Kingbird J-2, while the second prototype became the J-3, a six-seat mailplane, with 300hp engines.

Production

In total, 19 Kingbirds were built between 1929 and 1931, comprising one Kingbird C prototype, two Kingbird D-1 prototypes (later converted to D-2s), 14 production Kingbird D-2s, one King D-3 executive transport and one RC-1 for the USMC.

Technical data – King Bird C, D-2 and D-3	
ENGINE	(C) Two 185hp Curtiss Challenger; (D-2) two 300hp Wright Whirlwind J-6-9; (D-3) two 330hp Whirlwind R-975E (J-6-9)
WINGSPAN	54ft 6in
LENGTH	34ft 5⅛in
HEIGHT	10ft
WING AREA	405 sq/ft
EMPTY WEIGHT	(C) 3,442lb; (D-2) 3,877lb; (D-3) 4,215lb
GROSS WEIGHT	(C) 5,202lb; (D-2) 6,115lb; (D-3) 6,600lb
MAX SPEED	(C) 113mph; (D-2 and 3) 142mph
SERVICE CEILING	(C) 12,900ft; (D-2 and 3) 16,000ft
MAX RANGE	(C) 378 miles; (D-2) 415 miles; (D-3) 550 miles
ACCOMMODATION	(C) one pilot, six passengers; (D-2) one pilot, seven passengers; (D-3) one pilot, five passengers.

Only 14 Curtiss Kingbird D2s were built between 1929 and 1931, and the only customer was Eastern Air Transport. A useful aircraft with several unusual design features, the Kingbird achieved very little success because of its launch at the beginning of the Great Depression.

Thrush (Model 56) T

Development
Just like the Kingbird, the Thrush (Model 56) was launched at the wrong time, right at the beginning of the Great Depression.

Design
Effectively a six-seat version of the highly successful Robin, the Thrush was built in two versions; the first, indicating the type of engine installed, was named the Challenger Thrush. The fuselage of the Thrush was virtually all riveted aluminium tubing in place of welded steel. Early testing revealed the aircraft to be underpowered and a streamlined, close-fitting cowling around the engine did little to improve its performance. The first prototype, registered 7568 (c/n G-1), was used to test a horn-balanced rudder. The main production model, the Thrush J, was powered by a 225hp Wright J-6-7 Whirlwind engine.

Service
The Challenger Thrush first flew in 1929, the variant being presented to the general public with a price tag of $10,000. The first two aircraft, 7568 and 9787 (c/n G-2), were converted to Thrush J standard. Even with the 225hp Whirlwind installed, the Thrush was still underpowered, while the type's two

The most famous Thrush was NC7568 *Outdoor Girl* (ex-prototype G-1 and 7568) in which Helen Richey and Francis Marsalis remained airborne for ten days straight in December 1929.

main competitors, the Ryan Brougham and Travel Air 6000, both had a power advantage of almost 200hp. All ten production aircraft were given the civilian registrations 522N, 523N, 542N, 552N, 553N, 562N and 580582N (c/n 10011010). 562N crashed on its maiden flight and its registration was transferred to c/n 1007.

One Thrush hit the headlines between December 20 and 30, 1933, when Helen Richey and Frances Harrell Marsalis remained airborne for 237hrs 43mins in NC7568 *Outdoor Girl* by using air-to-air refuelling. The plan was to stay aloft until January 1, 1934, but even so, the old record was broken by 196hrs. NC7658, the prototype, was reregistered as YV-EBU, and sold to Venezuela in June 1940. It was most likely the last survivor of this rare breed.

Production
In total, 13 aircraft were built, comprising three Challenger Thrush prototypes built at Garden City, two of which were later converted to "J" standard, and ten production Thrush J, all of which were built at St Louis.

Technical data – Thrush J	
ENGINE	One 225hp Wright J-6-7 Whirlwind
WINGSPAN	48ft
LENGTH	32ft 7½in
HEIGHT	9ft 3in
WING AREA	305sq/ft
EMPTY WEIGHT	2,260lb
MAX TAKE-OFF WEIGHT	3,678lb
MAX SPEED	122mph at sea level
CLIMB RATE	650ft/min
SERVICE CEILING	13,200ft
RANGE	493 miles on 60 gallons of fuel
ACCOMMODATION	One pilot and five passengers

Curtiss-Wright Miscellaneous

On July 5, 1929, 12 companies merged simultaneously, all of which were owned by the Curtiss Aeroplane and Motor Company of Buffalo, New York, and by Wright Aeronautical of Dayton Ohio. Together they created the largest aircraft company in the US: Curtiss-Wright. The previous year, Curtiss had bought Robertson Airlines of St Louis, Missouri, to create the Curtiss-Robertson Aircraft Corporation, specifically to build aircraft. The aircraft were designed at other Curtiss-owned establishments, but it was not long before machines were designed in both St Louis and in Wichita, the home of Travel Air, which was bought by Curtiss in 1929. Both Curtiss-Robertson and Travel Air were part of the merger that created the Curtiss-Wright Company, and many subsequent designs were prefixed with CW.

However, not all designs followed this route; the CA-1 biplane amphibian designed by British test pilot Frank Courtney was one good example, as were the Curtiss-Robinson CR-1 Skeeter and CR-2 Coupe – the former was an ultralight and the latter a two-seat cabin monoplane.

The first Curtiss-Wright machine was the CW-1 Junior, which was effectively an improved Skeeter powered by a 45hp Szekely engine and priced at $1,490. A quiet success story, 261 Juniors were sold, as well as one CW-1A with a 40hp Augustine rotary, and two CW-1Bs with a 40hp Salmson radial. A further development of the Junior was the CW-3 Duckling, an amphibious version with a 60hp Velie radial, which was later replaced by the CW-3W and CW-3L with a 90hp Warner or Lambert radial. The designation CW-2 was an unbuilt project, while CW-4 was applied to the T-32 Condor and/or the Travel Air 4000. The CW-5 was an unbuilt freighter and CW-6 to CW-11 were allocated to former Travel Air models.

The two-seat biplane CW-12 Sport Trainer spawned a number of developments including the high-performance CW-12K and the CW-12Q, which was the most successful, with 27 examples sold. CW-13 was not taken up, but the CW-14 was a development of the Travel Air 4000/4, which was originally

Designed by Frank Courtney, the CA-1 Amphibian was a good-looking aircraft powered by a 365hp Wright R-975E radial. Only three were built, all of which were sold to Japan.

named the Speedwing. The name Osprey, a two-seat military export version, was also applied to the CW-14. A single 185hp Challenger-powered CW-14C prototype was built and resulted in three CW-A14D three-seaters being sold with 240hp Whirlwind engines. The CW-B14B Speedwing Deluxe was even more powerful with a 300hp Whirlwind, although only two were built, followed by a single two-seat CW-B14R Special Speedwing Deluxe with a 420hp super-charged engine. One military CW-14B and one CW-C14R were built, followed by the CW-15 Sedan, which was very similar to the Travel Air Model 10 andt resulted in 15 orders.

A three-seat version of the CW-12, named the CW-17 Light Sport, was marketed in three different versions; the CW-16E (ten were built), the CW-16K (11 were built) and the CW-16W (one was built). Finally, a 420hp version of the CW-B14B was designed under the name CW-17R Pursuit Osprey but it is not clear whether a prototype was built, and the CW-18 was a planned trainer for the USAAC.

Above left: An improved version of the Curtiss-Robinson CR-1 Skeeter, the CR-1 Junior ultralight was a popular recreational aircraft, which cost $1,490.

Above right: The CW-14 was a development of the Travel Air 4000/4 and produced several variants including this CW-B14D Osprey.

Below left: Another CW-14 variant was the CW-B14B Speedwing Deluxe powered by a 240hp Wright J-6-7 (R-760E Whirlwind) engine; only two were built.

Below right: Designed by an ex-Travel Air employee, the CW-15 Sedan resembled the Travel Air Model 10. Fifteen were built in three variants, each with a different engine.

A-8/-10/-12 Shrike (Model 59/60)

Development

The US Army attack bomber requirement, issued in 1929, instigated designs by Atlantic-Fokker in the shape of the XA-7, and Curtiss with its XA-8. It was the latter that was selected, an aircraft that would go on to become the USAAC's main attack aircraft for the majority of the 1930s.

Design

Designed by Don Berlin, the A-8 "Shrike" was an impressive aircraft that featured a large number of advances and firsts for Curtiss as well as ideas that dated back to World War One. The aircraft was the first all-metal, low-wing monoplane to be built by Curtiss. It was fitted with advancements such as leading-edge slots and trailing-edge flaps but was also installed with strut and wire-braced wings, which, with the exception of the Douglas O-31 and Boeing P-36, had not been seen since World War One.

The pilot and an observer/gunner were positioned in widely spaced cockpits, the former under a fully enclosed canopy (only for the XA-8, all other variants were open) and the latter only protected by an extended windscreen. Power for the XA-8 and the production YA-8 (Model 59A) and Y1A-8 was provided by a 600hp Curtiss V-1570C inline engine with a radiator below the nose. However, the experimental YA-10 (Model 49B) was powered by a Pratt & Whitney R-1690-9 Hornet radial. The radial engine was the preference of the US Navy, especially for carrier-borne operations, and the resulting production order was for the A-12 (Model 60). Still fitted with open cockpits, the A-12 had the rear cockpit moved much closer to the pilot in order to improve communications.

Service

The XA-8 prototype was first flown in June 1931 and was followed by the first of eight service test aircraft, which joined the USAAC from April 1932. Serving with the 13th Attack Squadron, 3rd Attack Group at Fort Crockett, Texas, the A-8 took the USAAC by storm, the service up until then having only operated biplanes. The main production variant, the A-12, entered service from 1934 with the 8th and 18th Attack Squadron, 3rd Attack Group. At least nine A-12s were operational at Hickam Field during the attack on Pearl Harbor and the type remained in service until 1942.

In addition, 20 A-12s joined the Chinese Nationalist Force in May 1936, serving with the 27th and 28th Squadrons, 9th Group, but after some initial success, very few survived the Japanese onslaught in the summer of 1937 when hostilities broke out there.

Production

One XA-8 prototype (30-387) was built, followed by five YA-8 (serial numbers 32-34432–348) and eight Y1A-8 (serial numbers 32-34932–356) service test aircraft; 12 of the service test machines were redesignated A-8. The first YA-8 was converted to the YA-10 and another to the XS2C-1 Shrike (Model 69), which became the first two-seat combat monoplane to be evaluated by the US Navy since the early 1920s. The main production variant was the A-12, of which 46 were built (33-21233–257), at a cost of $19,483 each, minus GFE. Twenty A-12s (c/n 12155–12174) were sold to China and deliveries commenced from May 1936 at a cost of $24,328.45 each.

Technical data – A-12 Shrike	
ENGINE	One 690hp Wright R-1820-21 Cyclone
WINGSPAN	44ft
LENGTH	32ft 3in
HEIGHT	9ft 4in
WING AREA	284sq/ft
EMPTY WEIGHT	3,898lb
MAX-TAKEOFF WEIGHT	5,756lb
MAX SPEED	177mph at sea level
SERVICE CEILING	15,150ft
RANGE	510 miles
ARMAMENT	Five 0.30in machine guns, four with limited adjustment in landing gear fairings and one, ring mounted for observer, plus provision for four 122lb bombs or ten 30lb bombs on underwing racks

Above: The prototype XA-8, 30-387, named the "Shrike," made an impact on the attack capability of the USAAC during the mid-1930s.

Right: A Curtiss A-8 Shrike of the 13th Attack Squadron during evaluation by the USAAC, which resulted in a 46-strong order for the A-12.

F9C Sparrowhawk (Model 58)

Development

A US Navy requirement for a small fighter to operate from its new giant rigid airships in 1930 resulted in a competition between the Atlantic-Fokker XFA-1, the Berliner-Joyce XFJ-1 and the Curtiss XF9C-1 (Model 58). The fighter was not to be installed with folding wings so the dimensions would be small. However, the US Navy was not impressed with any of the designs; the USS *Akron* (ZRS-4) had a hangar within its huge hull capable of holding four fighters, known as "parasite fighters." These aircraft could be launched and retrieved via a trapeze, which lifted and lowered the fighter through the bottom of the airship.

Design

With a span of just 25ft 6in, the XF9C-1 was selected to equip the US Navy's main rigid airships, the USS *Akron* and USS *Macon* (ZRS-5). The XF9C-1 had a metal monocoque fuselage and tail, while the metal wings were covered in fabric, with power provided by a 420hp Wright R-975C Whirlwind. A second prototype, the XF9C-2 (Model 58A), was built with a more simplistic undercarriage, which had single struts and wheel spats. This aircraft was powered by the production engine, a 438hp R-975E-3, and the production F9C-2 Sparrowhawk differed from the two prototypes by having an upper gull wing instead of a flat wing, which attached directly to the upper fuselage.

Service

The XF9C-1, serialled A8731, was ordered by the US Navy on June 30, 1930 and first flew on February 12, 1931. Installed with airship hook-up gear at the Naval Aircraft Factory, A8731 was trialled with the USS *Los Angeles* in October 1931. Only six production machines were ordered in October 1931, and the first of them, 9056, was flown on April 14, 1932. The F9C-2 began service with the USS *Akron* from September 1932 and post-service modifications included a repositioned rudder post and slightly increased rudder area. The USS *Akron* was lost in 1933 without any Sparrowhawks on board and those allocated to it were transferred to the USS *Macon*. During service with the *Macon*, the Sparrowhawks regularly operated without an undercarriage and used a 30-gallon auxiliary fuel tank to extend the little fighter's range. The USS *Macon* was lost in 1935, this time taking all four Sparrowhawks down to the seabed with it.

During their short service, the brightly coloured Sparrowhawks captured the imagination of the US public in their novel role as a "parasite fighter," protecting the giant mother ship. The first prototype was scrapped in January 1935 and the two surviving F9C-2s suffered the same fate in 1936 and 1937. Only the second prototype, XF9C-2, is preserved at the Smithsonian's Steven F Udvar-Hazy Center, Virginia.

Production

One XF9C-1 (A8731) prototype was built, plus one XF9C-2 (X986M) prototype and six production F9C-2 Sparrowhawks (9056-9061), the latter at a cost of $24,426 each, minus GFE.

Technical data – F9C Sparrowhawk	
ENGINE	One 438hp Wright R-975E-3 Whirlwind
WINGSPAN	25ft 6in
LENGTH	20ft 1½in
HEIGHT	10ft 7in (with skyhook)
WING AREA	172.80sq/ft
EMPTY WEIGHT	2,089lb
MAX-TAKEOFF WEIGHT	2,779lb
MAX SPEED	176mph at 4,000ft
SERVICE CEILING	19,200ft
RANGE	297 miles
ARMAMENT	Two fixed synchronized forward-firing 0.30in Browning machine guns

Considering there were only ever six Sparrowhawks built, the fighter had a novel method of operating from an airship, which made it one of the most well-known types of the early to mid-1930s.

The prototype, XF9C-1, serialled A8731, which was first flown in February 1931. This aircraft alone cost $74,442, minus GFE, and was retained by the Naval Aircraft Factory until it was scrapped in January 1935 with 213 flying hours to its credit.

Three of the USS *Macon*'s F9C-2 Sparrowhawks in 1934; four were lost (A9058–A9061) with the airship on February 12, 1935.

F11C and BFC-2 Goshawk and Hawk III (Model 64/67 and 68)

Development

Part of the long continuous story of the Curtiss Hawk family, the F11C, occasionally known as the Goshawk, was a development of the Hawk II (Model 35) and the Model 64A, which was ordered into US Navy production as the F11C. Only a few were built, and the model's service career was short.

Design

An improved derivative of the F6C (Model 34C), the XF11C-1 incorporated many major changes including a 600hp Wright R-1510-98 radial engine. The single strut undercarriage of the XF6C-5 and P-6E was fitted; the gap between the wings was slightly increased and all control surfaces were metal-covered. The second prototype, XF11C-2 (Model 64 [the current Hawk II demonstrator]), with a 700hp R-1820 Cyclone engine and fabric-covered control surfaces, would become the model for the production F11C-2 variant. The latter were redesignated as the BFC-2 in 1934 and the cockpit canopies were modified. Operated as fighter-bombers, the F11C-2 was fitted with a special crutch for dropping a single 500lb bomb in a dive. The fifth F11C-2 was delivered with a manually retracting undercarriage and metal frame wings and designated F11C-3 (Model 67). The subsequent production order was delivered as the BF2C-1 Goshawk (Model 67A) but vibration problems caused by the metal wings resulted in a short service career.

The export version of the BF2C-1 was the Hawk III (Model 68,) which was built with wooden wings and achieved orders from Thailand (delivered between August 1935 and February 1936), China (delivered between March 1936 and June 1938), Turkey and Argentina.

Service

Ordered in April 1932, the prototype XF11C-1, serialled 9217, was delivered to the US Navy in September 1932. The production F11C-2s were ordered in October 1932 and entered service in February 1933 with VF-1B aboard USS *Saratoga* (later changed to VB-2B and again to VB-3B). Redesignated as BFC-2s, the aircraft served the US Navy until early 1938. The BF2C-1s were delivered to VB-5B from October 1935 but, within a year, were withdrawn because of mechanical problems with the retractable undercarriage and vibration issues with the metal-framed wings.

Production

One XF11C-1 (Model 64) prototype and one XF11C-2 (Model 64A) prototype were built, followed by 28 production F11C-2s (later BFC-2) and 27 BF2C-1s. In total, 138 Hawk IIIs were built, made up of one demonstrator (Model 68A), registered as NR-14703, 24 to Siam (Thailand) (Model 68B), and 102 to China (Model 68C).

Technical data – F11C-2	
ENGINE	One 600hp Wright SR-1820F-2 Cyclone
WINGSPAN	31ft 6in
LENGTH	22ft 7in
HEIGHT	9ft 8½in
WING AREA	262sq/ft
EMPTY WEIGHT	3,037lb
MAX-TAKEOFF WEIGHT	4,132lb
MAX SPEED	202mph
SERVICE CEILING	21,100ft
RANGE	522 miles
ARMAMENT	Two fixed, synchronized, forward-firing 0.30in Browning machine guns, plus one 500lb bomb below fuselage, or four 112lb bombs on underwing racks

The prototype XF11C-1 (Model 64), 9217, which was delivered to the US Navy for evaluation in September 1932. The cost of the single machine was $65,306.18.

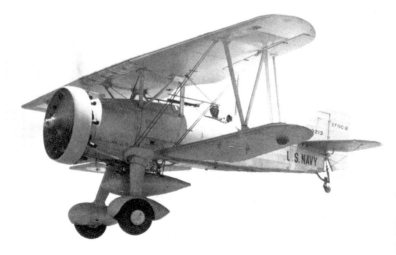

The 700hp Wright R-1820 Cyclone-powered XF11C-2 prototype, serialled 9213, was the template for the production machines.

T-32 Condor II (CW-4)

Development
The T-32 was a little out of place when it first appeared in 1933 in comparison to the sleek, fast monoplane airliners that were beginning to appear. It had a biplane configuration, tubby fuselage and slow speed. However, the aircraft, named "Condor II" was easy to build, competitively priced and was destined to pioneer night-sleeper travel, taking advantage of its spacious fuselage.

Design
The T-32 had a strut-braced single fin and rudder assembly. The fuselage was the old-fashioned tubular frame, covered in fabric and the wings contained tubular wing spars, which were used in the original Condors. The only modern feature of the T-32 was the undercarriage, which retracted into the rear of the engine nacelles. The general internal layout of the T-32 was a luxurious 12-passenger night sleeper, although some examples were modified for 15 passengers in a standard seating arrangement.

The bomber variant, the BT-32, was capable of carrying up to 1,680lbs of bombs in the fuselage or on racks under the wings. Machine gun positions were created above the nose, two in the mid-fuselage and one in the rear cabin floor.

Several variants of the T-32 were built, including the AT-32A, B and C with variable-pitch propellers and NACA cowlings around the SGR-1820-F2 engines. The AT-32D was installed with SGR-1820-F3 engines and all four built were converted to 15-seaters. The AT-32E served the US Navy and USMC as the R4C-1 as a "deluxe" 12-seater, while the CT-32 had a three-segment loading door in the starboard and was used for cargo operations. The designation YC-30 was applied to a pair of T-32s, which were bought by the US Army and used as executive transport.

Service
Built in the recently re-opened St Louis plant, the first Condor made its maiden flight on January 30, 1933. At a retail price of $60,000, several Condors were purchased by American Airways and Eastern Air Transport; the latter operated the aircraft for almost three years on its night sleep routes. Two YC-30s were operated by the USAAC until 1938 and one T-32 was converted with extra

The prototype BT-32 bomber, destined to be sold to China, demonstrates the underwing bomb load under the starboard wing only for the benefit of the camera.

long-range tanks, floats or skis for the Byrd Antarctic Expedition in 1933. The US Navy used its R4C-1s for a US Antarctic Survey and one of the aircraft was abandoned there in 1941.

All eight of the BT-32 bombers served with foreign air forces; one went to China, three seaplane versions went to Columbia and four to the Peruvian Air Force, which did not retire the type until 1956. The three cargo-carrying CT-32s were sold to Argentina.

Production

A total of 45 "Condor IIs" were built between 1932 and October 1934; they comprised 21 12-passenger sleepers, two of these served as YC-30s (33-320 and 33-321); ten aircraft were modified to AT-32 standard (redesignated T-32C); four AT-32As, three AT-32Bs, one AT-32C, four AT-32Ds and two AT-32Es (R4C-1), eight BT-32s and three CT-32s.

Technical data – BT-32 and AT-32 Condor II	
ENGINE	(BT) Two 710hp Wright SCR-1820-F3 Cyclone; (AT) two 720hp Wright R-1820F Cyclone
WINGSPAN	82ft
LENGTH	(BT) 48ft 7in; (AT) 49ft 6in
HEIGHT	16ft 4in
WING AREA	(BT) 1,276sq/ft; (AT) 1,208sq/ft
EMPTY WEIGHT	(BT (equipped)) 11,233lb; (AT) 12,235lb
GROSS WEIGHT	(BT (max take-off) 17,500lb; (AT) 17,500lb
MAX SPEED	(BT) 176mph; (AT) 190mph
SERVICE CEILING	(BT) 22,000ft; (AT) 23,000ft
MAX RANGE	(BT) 840 miles; (AT) 716 miles
ARMAMENT	(BT) five flexible 0.3in machine guns and up to 1,680lb of bombs
ACCOMMODATION	(AT) two pilots, cabin attendant and up to 15 passengers

One of three float-equipped BT-32 Condors, which served with the Columbian Air Force.

SOC Seagull (Model 71)

Development

In a service career that virtually mirrored the Fairey Swordfish, the SOC "Seagull," like its British counterpart, originated in 1933, and was obsolete by the beginning of World War Two but still served longer than the aircraft intended to replace it. The SOC (Model 71) was the result of competition for a US Navy requirement for a new scouting/observation (SO) aircraft. Douglas and Vought also presented proposals but, surprisingly, it was the traditionally-built SOC that was ordered by the US Navy on June 19, 1933.

Design

The basic construction of the SOC was tube and fabric and the only "modern" features it displayed were full-span leading edge slats on the upper mainplane, trailing edge flaps on the upper mainplane and a substantial cowling around the engine. The prototype had an amphibious undercarriage, which comprised a large central float that incorporated a twin wheel retractable landing gear. Production aircraft were built as pure seaplanes with the option of a fixed main undercarriage and tailwheel; either option was not difficult to apply. The wings (which could be folded) and the tail unit were made of light alloy. The fuselage was welded steel tube covered by aluminium and fabric. Both the pilot and observer/gunner operated from tandem cockpits under a transparent canopy. The upper rear fuselage or "turtleback" could be retracted to improve the field of fire to the rear.

Service

The XO3C-1 prototype first flew in April 1934 and the first SOC-1s entered service with USS *Marblehead* on November 12, 1935. The first units to receive the type were VS-5B, VS-6B, VS-9S, VS-10S, VS-11S and VS-12S with deliveries continuing to 1938, by which time the SOC was prolific

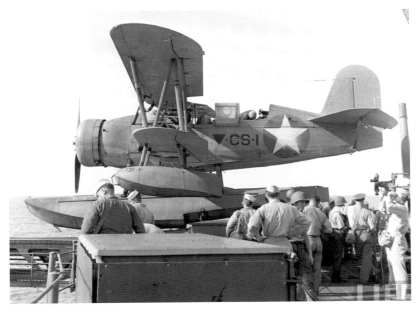

A SOC-1 on the catapult of a US Navy cruiser in July 1942, by which time, the Seagull should have been in the twilight of its operational career.

throughout the US Navy. By 1941, the US Navy was steadily re-equipping its SOC fleet with the Vought Kingfisher and it was expected, the SOC Seagull (only known by this name from 1941) would be replaced by the SO3C "Seamew." The latter proved to be a failure, giving the US Navy no choice other than to re-establish the Seagull back into operational units from 1943 onwards, where it continued to serve for the remainder of the war. As Kingfisher production increased, the Seagull was eventually replaced but still continued to serve in the second line as trainers and general communications aircraft until removed from the inventory in 1945.

Production

In total, 322 SOC Seagulls were built, 258 of them SOC-1 to SOC-4 by Curtiss, and 64 SOC-3 (SON-1) by the Naval Aircraft Factory, Philadelphia, Pennsylvania.

Technical data – SOC-1 Seaplane	
ENGINE	One 600hp Pratt & Whitney R-1340-18 Wasp
WINGSPAN	36ft
LENGTH	26ft 6in
HEIGHT	14ft 9in
WING AREA	342sq/ft
EMPTY WEIGHT	3,788lb
MAX TAKE-OFF WEIGHT	5,437lb
MAX SPEED	165mph at 5,000ft
SERVICE CEILING	14,900ft
MAX RANGE	675 miles
ARMAMENT	Two 0.30in machine guns, one fixed and one flexible, plus external racks for 650lb of bombs

Curtiss SOC-1, 9877, of the Cruisers Scouting Force, US Navy, one of 135 examples that were built.

Hawk 75/P-36 (Model 75)

Development

When the Curtiss Model 75 first appeared in April 1935, it represented a pivotal moment in the history of Curtiss and the US fighter aircraft industry as a whole. Designed by Donovan Reese Berlin, the Model 75 drew nothing from Curtiss' long experience in designing and building fighter aircraft.

Design

The fighter was a low-wing cantilever monoplane with an aluminium alloy semi-monocoque fuselage and multi-spar all-metal wing, both of which were covered in Alclad knitted together with flush rivets. A retractable undercarriage, hydraulically-activated flaps and a fully enclosed cockpit with an aft opening canopy were features of the Model 75, which made it a state-of-the-art machine and one of the most advanced fighters of its day. However, fighter development across the world began to accelerate across the world from the mid-1930s and within two years of the Model 75 entering service, aspects of its performance were already inferior. Highly manoeuvrable with pleasant handling characteristics, the Model 75 soon lacked the vital climb-and-dive, acceleration and level speed that determine success in the early stages of World War Two.

Service

Despite losing a US Army pursuit competition against the Seversky P-35, Curtiss would sell more Model 75s over its competitor; 277 were sold to the USAAC as P-36s alone. Another 753, designated as the Hawk 75A, were sold overseas; and the biggest order came from France for 300 (later rising to 316) aircraft. France ordered the Hawk 75A with a Pratt & Whitney Twin Wasp engine (A-1 to A-3) and a Wright Cyclone powerplant (A-4). Many aircraft did not reach France before it fell to Germany in June 1940, so these were transferred to the RAF as the Mohawk Mk III (Wasp) and Mohawk Mk IV (ex-A4 Cyclone).

In total, 236 Mohawks eventually entered RAF service from December 1914 when No 5 Squadron was re-equipped at Dum Dum, Calcutta. Nos 146 and 155 Squadrons (until January 1944) also operated the Mohawk in the Far East, as did No 3 (SAAF) Squadron and No 41 (SAAF) Squadron in North Africa.

Originally ordered by the USAAC as a P-36A, 38-191 was delivered as a P-36C, a variant that featured an extra 0.30in machine gun in each wing and external ammunition boxes below the wing. This aircraft was written off on March 18, 1943, four miles east of El Paso, Texas.

In French service, the II/4 Groupe de Chasses were credited with scoring the first Allied victories of World War Two when two Bf109Es were brought down on September 8, 1939. Those machines that survived the German invasion were later used by the Vichy French in North Africa but suffered heavy losses. In USAAC service, the P-36A joined the 20th Pursuit Group at Barksdale Field in April 1938 but a catalogue of teething problems effectively ended the type's career at a very early stage. Relegated to training duties, a batch of 39 P-36As was delivered to Hawaii by the USS *Enterprise* in February 1941. Five of this group were airborne during the Pearl Harbour attack, shooting down a pair of A6M2 Zeros for the loss of one P-36A. These were among the earliest US airborne victories of the war.

Technical data – Wellington III	
ENGINE	One 875hp Wright GR-1820-G3
SPAN	37ft
LENGTH	28ft 7in
HEIGHT	9ft 3in
WING AREA	236sq/ft
EMPTY WEIGHT	3,975lb
MAX TAKE-OF WEIGHT	5,305lb
MAX SPEED	280mph at 10,000ft
CEILING	31,800ft
ARMAMENT	Two wing-mounted 0.30in machine guns and two fuselage-mounted 0.30in or 0.50in machine guns

Curtiss P-36Cs of the 27th Pursuit Squadron, 1st Fighter Group, pictured en route to the National Air Races at Cleveland, Ohio, in early September 1939. The unit only operated the type during 1939 and the unusual "non-standard" pre-war camouflage was applied for war games, which had only taken place a few weeks earlier.

An RAF Mohawk IV, which was a Hawk 75A-4 powered by a Cyclone engine, receives attention in Burma in 1943. Diverted from a large French order, the Mohawk provided the RAF with a "good enough" fighter to help slow the advance of the Japanese in the Far East.

CW-19/23

Development

The CW-19 was designed by George Page in late 1934 following a request from the Bureau of Air Commerce encouraging the US aircraft industry to build new lightweight private aircraft, and taking full advantage of the latest construction techniques. Developed as a private aircraft from the outset, the design better lent itself to that of a military machine and the little success the CW-19 to achieve was in this market.

Design

Page's initial design was designated CW-19L "Coupé" and was a two-seat, side-by-side arrangement, low-wing cabin monoplane. The CW-19L was powered by a 90hp Lambert R-266 engine driving a Curtiss fixed-pitch propeller. A single CW-19W, with the same configuration as that of its predecessor, was fitted with a 145hp Warner Super Scarab but its performance was deemed to be too high for a civilian pilot.

The military version, the CW-19R, saw the coupé-type cabin replaced by a tandem arrangement under a long sliding canopy. Armament options included a single synchronized machine gun firing through the propeller, plus the option for two more mounted on the outside of the substantial fixed undercarriage fairings. One machine gun could be flexibly mounted in the rear cockpit and bomb racks could be fitted under the fuselage.

A development of the CW-19R, only one CW-23 was produced as a company-owned prototype. Powered by a 600hp Pratt & Whitney R-1340 Wasp, the aircraft featured a retractable undercarriage and was designed to serve the USAAC as a basic combat trainer. First flown in 1939 with the civilian registration NX19427, the CW-23 was evaluated by the military, but no orders were forthcoming.

Service

First flown in 1935, the CW-19L was purchased by the US government and registered as NS-69. In the CW-19R, Curtiss was confident that the aircraft could be used as a utility fighter capable of reconnaissance or ground-attack operations. However, only 23 aircraft were sold to Bolivia, China, Cuba, the Dominican Republic and Ecuador. These few aircraft gave good service. Ecuador did not retire the type until 1943, followed by Cuba in 194,8 and Bolivia in 1949. Only one ex-Bolivian Air Force CW-19R survives today.

Production

In total, 29 aircraft were built, made up of one CW-19L, one CW-19W, 23 CW-19R, three CW-A19R and one CW-23.

Technical data – CW-19R	
ENGINE	One 350hp Wright R-760E2 Whirlwind
WINGSPAN	35ft
LENGTH	26ft 4in
HEIGHT	8ft 2in
WING AREA	174sq/ft
EMPTY WEIGHT	1,992lb
MAX TAKE-OFF WEIGHT	3,500lb
MAX SPEED	185mph
CLIMB RATE	1,890 ft/min
ARMAMENT	One fixed, forward-firing 0.303in machine gun with provision for one mounted in the rear cockpit and two more on outer sides of wheel fairings, plus light bombs on under-fuselage racks

Cuban Air Force CW-19R "50" pictured in Miami in 1940 for maintenance. Cuba operated the CW-19R from 1937 to 1948.

XA-14 and A-18 Shrike II (Model 76)

Development

The Curtiss Model 76 was a company venture to produce a two-seat, twin-engine ground attack aircraft, which was launched in parallel with the Hawk 75 prototype. A single prototype, designated the XA-14, was built with the hope of large orders for the production machine, the A-18 Shrike II.

Design

The Model 76 was a mid-wing cantilever monoplane of all metal construction, with the exception of all of the control surfaces and the wing aft of the front spar, which was covered in fabric. The undercarriage was retractable, although the main wheels remained partially exposed. A very aerodynamic design, both crew were accommodated in a pair of smooth glazed cockpits, which blended into the upper fuselage. An internal bomb bay was large enough to hold 600lb of bombs and four 0.30in machine-guns were mounted in the nose and one was flexibly mounted for the observer. The Model 76 was powered by a pair of Wright XR-1510 engines while production machines were fitted with Wright Cyclones.

A Pratt & Whitney R-1830-powered improved Model 76B was offered to the USAAC, as was a similar export version but neither received any interest.

Service

The Model 76 was first flown in September 1935 and, after an evaluation by the USAAC at Wright Field, was returned to Curtiss and fitted with the more powerful 775hp Wright R-1670-5 Cyclones with constant-speed propellers. Redesignated by the USAAC as the XA-14, an order was placed for 13 production aircraft designated Y1A-18 and named "Shrike II" by Curtiss in July 1936. The Y1A-18 was a refined version of the original XA-14 with more powerful engines and part of the bomb load was spread into extra bays in the wings.

Economic reasons prevented the USAAC from ordering more Shrikes, all of which were assigned to the 8th Attack Squadron, 3rd Attack Group, Barksdale Field, Louisiana, in 1937. Pioneers of low-flying formation attacks on ground targets, the Shrike II proved to be a good airplane but suffered from a weak undercarriage, which claimed eight aircraft by 1941 when they were simply designated as A-18s. The survivors were transferred to the Caribbean Air Force in late 1941. Twelve months later, only three remained airworthy, the type clinging on until early 1943 when a lack of spares forced the Shrike II's retirement.

Production

One XA-14 (Model 76) serialled X15314, and 13 Y1A-18s (Model 76A) serialled 12187–12199, at a cost of $104,640 each were produced and were delivered between July 1936 and October 1937.

Technical data – A-18	
ENGINE	Two 850hp Wright R-1820-47 Cyclone
WINGSPAN	59ft 6in
LENGTH	41ft
HEIGHT	11ft 6in
WING AREA	526sq/ft
EMPTY WEIGHT	9,410lb
MAX-TAKEOFF WEIGHT	13,170lb
MAX SPEED	247mph
SERVICE CEILING	28,650ft
RANGE	651 miles
ARMAMENT	Five 0.3in machine-guns, plus 600lb of bombs

A very useful ground attack aircraft, which was only let down by a weak undercarriage, a lack of funds prevented the USAAC from ordering considerably more than the 13 that entered service.

SBC Helldiver (Model 77)

Development
The story of the second Curtiss aircraft to be named Helldiver began in 1932 when the US Navy placed an order for a two-seat fighter designated the XF12C-1 (Model 73). First flown in 1933, the XF12C-1 was a parasol-wing monoplane with a retractable undercarriage and powered by a Wright Whirlwind engine. By the end of 1933, the US Navy had decided to use the aircraft in a scout role and finally as a scout bomber. The aircraft was subsequently lost in September 1934 during a dive test; the parasol arrangement was clearly not suitable for dive bombing. As a result, a new biplane prototype was ordered as the XSBC-2 Helldiver was born (Model 77).

Design
The XSBC-2 was a conventional design of mixed construction; the fuselage and tail surfaces were metal monocoque, the wings were metal framed the upper mainplane was metal-covered and the lower mainplane was covered in fabric. Ailerons, elevators and rudder were fabric-covered and full span flaps were fitted to the lower mainplane. The pilot and observer/air gunner were accommodated in tandem under a long canopy and a rear turtle deck, similar to those that were fitted to the earlier SOC, could be collapsed to improve the rearward field of fire.

The XSBC-2 was powered by a 700hp Wright R-1510 Whirlwind, which was later replaced by XR-1510-12. Neither was satisfactory but when the 700hp Pratt & Whitney R-1535-82 Twin Wasp Junior became available in March 1936, the aircraft was redesignated to XSBC-3 (Model 77A) and a production order for 83 aircraft was placed by the US Navy on August 29, 1936.

Service
The first 83 production SBC-3 Helldivers were delivered to the US NAVY on July 17, 1937. VS-5 was the first unit to receive the type aboard USS *Yorktown*, the remainder all served with carrier-based units until late 1941, by which time the type had been relegated to second-line duties. One of the late production SBC-3s served as the prototype for the XSBC-4 (Model 77B), which was powered by the 850hp Wright R-1820-34 Cyclone. A contract for 174 production SBC-4s was placed on January 5, 1938, with deliveries commencing in March 1939. By that time, the US Navy had finally acknowledged that the era of the combat biplane was over and many of the SBC-4s were delivered direct to reserve units. Two US Navy SBC-4 units were still operational at the time of Pearl Harbor and the USMC retained a land-based SBC-4 unit until June 1943.

France ordered 90 SBC-4s in early 1940 but, to speed up the delivery, the US Navy released 50 of its own SBC-4s, which were refurbished and repainted in French markings and shipped across the Atlantic on the French carrier *Béarn*. However, mid-Atlantic, France capitulated to Germany, and the carrier diverted to Martinique where the SBC-4s were eventually scrapped. Five aircraft, intended for France made their way to Britain via Canada to be renamed by the RAF as Cleveland Mk I. One was destroyed in an air raid while the remainder became instructional airframes.

Production
One prototype, designated XSBC-2 (Model 77) and re-designated XSBC-3, followed by 83 SBC-3s (Model 77A) and 174 SBC-4s were built.

Technical data – SBC-4 Helldiver	
ENGINE	One 900hp Wright R-1820-34 Cyclone 9
WINGSPAN	34ft
LENGTH	28ft 1½in
HEIGHT	10ft 5in
WING AREA	317sq/ft
EMPTY WEIGHT	4,552lb
MAX TAKE-OFF WEIGHT	7,080lb
MAX SPEED	234mph at 15,200ft
SERVICE CEILING	24,000ft
MAX RANGE	400 miles with a 500lb bomb
ARMAMENT	Two 0.3in machine guns, one forward-firing and on a flexible mount, plus one 500lb bomb

The RAF took delivery of five SBC-4s in August 1941 and renamed them Cleveland Mk I, serialled AA467–471. AA467 is pictured at Boscombe Down during trials by the Aeroplane & Armament Experimental Establishment (A&AEE).

Curtiss SBC-4 Helldiver, 1318, of the Seattle reserve on approach into Oakland in July 1940. (Bill Larkins)

Demon (Model CW-21)

Development

Intended as an economical yet high-performing fighter for countries with small military budgets, the CW-21 was a simple, minimally-equipped design, which was based on the CW-19. The wing of the latter was incorporated into a lightweight structure with only light armament, compared with European machines, and was not installed with self-sealing fuel tanks.

Design

An all-metal cantilever monoplane, the CW-21 featured a tail-wheel landing gear and rearward retracting main undercarriage units, which were concealed within underwing clamshell fairings because the wing was so thin. The lightweight frame of the prototype was powered by an 850hp Wright R-1820 engine, while the production CW-21 and CW-21Bs were powered by the 1,000hp version, which propelled it along at a maximum speed of 315mph and gave it a good climb rate of 4,500ft/min. The good performance was partly attributed to the lack of armour and of protection for the fuel tanks, plus a defensive armament of just two fuselage-mounted synchronized machine guns and the option of two more in the wings.

The CW-21A was only a proposal with Allison V-1710 engine, while the CW-21B featured a redesigned inward-retracting main undercarriage without the underwing fairings of the original machine.

Service

The first CW-21, NX19431, first flew on September 22, 1938, and, after being sold by the St Louis Airplane Division to the Curtiss-Wright Export Sales Division in February 1939, was despatched to China as a demonstrator. While there, test pilot Bob Fausel shot down a Japanese Air Force BR.20 bomber, which was attacking Chungking on April 4, 1939. The following month, the Chinese signed a contract for the prototype, three more CW-21s and 27 kits to be assembled by the Central Aircraft Manufacturing Company (CAMCO). The prototype was wrecked soon after and three CW-21s were

The first CW-21, wearing civilian registration NX19431, was first flown in September 1938. Sold to China in 1939, the aircraft was wrecked soon after.

delivered to China in May 1940 to later serve with the 1st AVG (Flying Tigers) until all three were lost on a ferry flight in December 1941.

In April 1940, the Dutch placed an order for 24 CW-21Bs, which were assembled in Java in February 1941 to serve with the 2nd Fighter Squadron, Netherlands East Indies Army Aviation Section. During early 1942, the CW-21Bs were heavily engaged against the overwhelming might of the Japanese Air Force and, despite scoring a few aerial victories, the vulnerability of the fighter soon saw the 24-strong fleet reduced to a handful of serviceable machines. At least one of the latter was captured by the Japanese.

Production

In total, 59 aircraft were built, comprising one prototype and three production CW-21s; 27 sets of components were sent to China and 24 CW-21Bs were sold to the Netherlands East Indies.

Technical data – CW-21B	
ENGINE	One 850hp Wright R-1820-G5 Cyclone
WINGSPAN	35ft
LENGTH	27ft 2½in
HEIGHT	8ft 2in
WING AREA	174.3 sq/ft
EMPTY WEIGHT	3,382lb
LOADED WEIGHT	4,500lb
MAX SPEED	314mph at 12,200ft
SERVICE CEILING	34,300ft
MAX RANGE	630 miles
ARMAMENT	Four machine guns of varying calibres and positions

The first of 24 production CW-21Bs, during flight testing in January 1941 with Bob Fausel at the controls.

SO3C Seagull/Seamew (Model 82)

Development

Designed in response to a US Navy requirement, issued in 1937, for a replacement for the SOC Seagull, which had just entered operational service, the SO3C "Seagull" was not a success, despite 795 being built. The US Navy's requirement was that the aircraft should be able to operate from ships at sea or land bases and, as such, could be quickly converted to a float or wheeled undercarriage arrangement. Prototype contracts were issued to Curtiss and Vought in May 1938, the former's aircraft being designated as the XS03C-1 (Model 82). While the design was far from perfect, it was Curtiss that won the production order.

Design

The SO3C was an all-metal aircraft with the exception of fabric-covered control surfaces, crewed by two accommodated in separated, fully enclosed cockpits. In the guise of a floatplane, a single large central float was balanced by a pair of strut-mounted wingtip stabilizer floats. As a landplane, the SO3C's undercarriage was fixed and characterized by a pair of large streamlined fairings. Power for the prototype was a 550hp Ranger XV-770-4, while production SO3C-1s (Model 82A) were fitted with a 520hp VX-770-6.

Instability problems plagued the S03C throughout its short career, the problem being partly cured by fitting upturned wingtips and increasing the area of the tail surfaces. The SO3C-2C "Seamew" was fitted with arrestor gear and the landplane version was capable of carrying a single 500lb bomb.

Service

The first SO3C-1s entered operational service with USS *Cleveland* in July 1942. However, the US Navy was not happy with the performance, handling or reliability of the Ranger engine, and it was not long before the SO3C was withdrawn from operational service to be replaced by the older SOC Seagull. Under the lend-lease scheme, the Federal Aviation Administration (FAA) ordered 250 SO3C-1Bs (Model 82C), which were renamed as the Seamew Mk I, a name later adopted by the US Navy. Only a fraction of the original number that the FAA ordered were ever delivered, and those that were served with 744 and 745 Squadrons at Yarmouth, Nova Scotia, and in Britain they served briefly with 700 and 755 Squadrons, based at Worthy Down, between October 1943 and October 1944. The Seamew was meant to re-equip the reformed 850 Squadron, the only operational unit based at Quonset Point, Rhode Island, on January 1, 1943, but the type was never received and squadron was disbanded after a month.

Several Seamews found a use as radio-controlled targets designated SO3C-1K, and in a final attempt to recover the situation Curtiss produced the SO3C-3 (Model 82C). Lightened and given more power, this variant did have marginally improved performance but, by early 1944, the US Navy had completely lost interest in the type.

Production

In total, 795 aircraft were built, made up of one XS03C-1 prototype; 141 SO3C-1 production aircraft; 30 SO3C-1K drones; 200 SO3C-2s; 59 Seamew Is (250 ordered), 250 SO3C-2Cs and 39 SO3C-3s (659 cancelled).

Technical data – XS03C-1 Seaplane and SO3C-2 Landplane	
ENGINE	(S) One 520hp Ranger V-770-6; (L) one 600hp Ranger V-770-6
WINGSPAN	38ft
LENGTH	(S) 35ft 11⅞in; (L) 35ft 8in
HEIGHT	(S) 15ft 3in; (L) 14ft 6in
WING AREA	275sq/ft
EMPTY WEIGHT	(S) 3,955lb; (L) 4,800lb
LOADED WEIGHT	(S) 5,365lb; (L) 7,200lb
MAX SPEED	(S) 190mph; (L) 172mph at 8,100ft
SERVICE CEILING	(S) 19,000ft; (L) 15,800ft
MAX RANGE	(S) 825 miles; (L) 1,150 miles
ARMAMENT	(S and L) two 0.30in machine guns, one fixed and one flexible and two 100lb bombs; (L) or two 325lb depth charges or one 500lb bomb

Right: Ranking as one the most unattractive Curtiss aircraft designs, the SO3C suffered from handling problems and an unreliable engine. Curtiss "Seamew" Mk I, FN475, is pictured during performance and handling trials by the A&AEE from Boscombe Down.

Below: A production SO3C-1 Seamew of the US Navy, which compared to the prototype, had redesigned wingtips and a larger vertical tail area.

C-46 Commando (CW-20)

Development

Originally built as a private venture to compete against the Boeing Stratoliner and Douglas DC-4, the Curtiss CW-20 36-seat airliner was designed for the civilian market but was destined to serve the military in large numbers across the globe.

Design

Designed in 1937 by George A Page, the main feature of the CW-20 was its "double-bubble" fuselage, which could withstand the pressure of high-altitude flying. The sides of the fuselage were creased at the point where the cabin floor fitted to the internal structure, creating two natural voids, one for cargo/baggage below and for passengers above. The prototype, CW-20T, was powered by a pair of 1,700hp Wright R-2600-C14-BA2 Twin Cyclones and featured a dihedral tailplane with endplate-type tail surfaces. The latter was later replaced by a single, large fin and rudder.

The first production variant for the USAAF was the CW-20A, which was virtually the same as the prototype. The last 21 built were delivered as CW-20Bs, and the military designation C-46A Commando was applied from then on. The C-46A was fitted with a large cargo door on the port side of the rear fuselage and had a strengthened floor and folding seats for up to 40 troops. Power was provided by a pair of Pratt & Whitney R-2800-43s, which gave better performance at higher altitudes over the prototype's Twin Cyclones.

The main production variant, the C-46D (CW-20B-2), had an extra door on the starboard side while the C-46E (CW-20B-3) was a utility variant with a stepped windscreen and three-blade Hamilton-Standard propellers. The C-46F (CW-20B-4) was a cargo variant with doors on both sides and squared off wingtips.

Service

The prototype CW-20, NX19426, was first flown by Edmund T Allen on March 26, 1940, and not long after was evaluated by the military with the temporary designation C-55. The military ordered 36 aircraft in September 1940, and the first them entered USAAF service in December 1941. Large numbers of C-47As were ordered, the type's high-altitude performance combined with a good load made it particularly useful in the CBI theatre where the famous over "The Hump" route kept troops supplied following the loss of the "Burma Road." In the Pacific theatre, the aircraft was used heavily by the USMC as the R5C-1, often to and from very rough landing strips. The C-46 also served in Europe from early 1945, alongside the C-47.

Post-war, the C-46 was not found to be suited to airliner operations and instead found a niche as a cargo transport while it remained in military use across the world. The type saw action in Korea and Vietnam and was not fully retired by the USAF until 1968. Several remain in civilian hands today, the best known are the three that served with Buffalo Airways in Canada – some of the "stars" of the TV series *Ice Pilots*.

Production

3181 C-46 Commandos were built between May 1942 and 1945; the main variants were the C-46A (1,039), C-46D (1,410), C-46E (17), C-46F (234) and R5C-1 (160).

Technical data – C-46A Commando	
ENGINE	Two 2,000hp Pratt & Whitney R-2800-51
WINGSPAN	108ft
LENGTH	76ft 4in
HEIGHT	21ft 9in
WING AREA	1,360 sq/ft
EMPTY WEIGHT	30,000lb
MAX TAKE-OFF WEIGHT	45,000lb
MAX SPEED	270mph at 15,000ft
SERVICE CEILING	24,500ft
RANGE	3,150 miles at 173mph
CAPACITY	Up to 50 troops, 33 stretcher patients and four attendants of 10,000lb of cargo

Right: One of more than 150 aircraft operated in airworthy condition by the Confederate Air Force, "The Tinker Belle" now named "China Doll" is a C-46F-1-CU Commando, which first saw service with Riddle Airlines.

Below: C-46A Commandoes of the 47th TCS (Troop Carrier Squadron), 313th TCG (Troop Carrier Group), 9th Air Force at Achiet, France, on March 21, 1945. Three days later, they dropped troops of the 17th Airborne Division across the Rhine during Operation *Varsity*.

XP-40, P-40 and Tomahawk Mk I (Model 81)

Development

There was no doubting that the P-63/Hawk 75 made quite an impression when it first appeared, but it was not destined to serve the USAAC in great numbers. There may have been some expectation that the next Curtiss fighter to be designed by Donovan Berlin's team would be even more impressive but, sadly for the USAAC and future USAAF, this was not to be.

Design

Rather than going back to the drawing board, Berlin produced the P-40, which was little more than a development of the P-36 rather than another state-of-the-art fighter. Curtiss was protecting the investment of time and money it had already put into the P-36 and presumed that, with little effort, the P-40 would be noticeably better. However, the result was only a modest improvement in performance, a distinct lack of agility and, from the mouths of those men who had to fight in them, a distinct disadvantage against all of the main adversaries. On the plus side, the P-40 retained the P-36's pleasant handling characteristics, was one of the most robust single-seat fighters of the entire war and was available in great numbers at a reasonable price. The P-40s were only armed with a pair of 0.30in machines guns in the wings and were delivered without armour, bullet-proof windscreens or self-sealing fuel tanks.

Service

The prototype, XP-40, which was the tenth production P-36 off the line, was first flown by test pilot Edward Elliot on October 14, 1938. Powered by an Allison V-1710 liquid-cooled engine, the aircraft was given the Curtiss designation Hawk 81A. Despite early misgivings, which mainly concerned the aircraft's disappointing performance, an order for 524 aircraft was placed by the USAAC on April 27, 1939. It first flew on April 4, 1940, and deliveries began in June 1940. The P-40 remained in USAAC/USAAF front-line service until October 1942 when the survivors were redesignated as RP-40s.

The first Tomahawk Mk Is arrived in Britain in November 1940 and went on to serve with 4, 16, 26, 168, 169, 231, 239, 241, 268, 349, 400, 403, 430 and 613 Squadrons and later several flights and OTUs until as late as 1944.

Production

One XP-40 (c/n 12424) was built, followed by 200 production P-40s (Model 81), although one (39-221) was converted to a P-40G (aka XP-40G). The production aircraft were given US Army serials. Another 140 Tomahawk Mk I (Model H81-A) were ordered and serialled AH741–880.

Technical data – XP-40	
ENGINE	One 1,150hp Allison V-1710-9
WINGSPAN	37ft 3½in
LENGTH	31ft 9³⁄₁₆in
HEIGHT	9ft 2¼in
WING AREA	236sq/ft
EMPTY WEIGHT	5,194lb
GROSS WEIGHT	6,280lb
MAX SPEED	327mph at 12,000ft
SERVICE CEILING	31,000ft
RANGE	470 miles at 70 percent power
ARMAMENT	Two 0.50in machine guns

Right: Brand new Curtiss P-40s rolling out of the Buffalo factory in the summer of 1940. Although only 199 were actually delivered to the USAAC, the original order of 524 aircraft, placed in April 1939, was, to date, the largest single order for fighters in the service's history.

Below: The RAF ordered 140 Tomahawk Mk Is but found that the fighter was lacking the performance to serve operationally, although it proved useful with Army Co-operation squadrons. AH769 is pictured at Boscombe Down prior to joining 268 Squadron and later 1686 Flight; the fighter remained with the latter until May 1944.

SB2C Helldiver (Model 84)

Development
The last of three Curtiss designs to bear the name Helldiver was the SB2C, which was destined to become the final aircraft built by the company for the US Navy and USMC and was by far the most extensively built.

Design
A low-wing cantilever monoplane, the SB2C was constructed of metal and featured folding wings so that it could be stored in aircraft carrier hangars. This latter requirement also dictated the aircraft's overall size, which was viewed by many as rather short for a dive bomber because it relied heavily on directional stability. Perforated trailing-edge flaps were split so that they doubled as dive-breaks. Wingtip leading-edge slats, roughly the same span as the ailerons, deployed automatically as the undercarriage was lowered so that the ailerons still remained effective at low speeds. The wide-track undercarriage was retractable and the semi-retractable tailwheel was steerable. Arrester gear was fitted to all models with the exception of the US Army's A-25, which also did not have folding wings.

Service
The prototype XSB2C-1, 1758, made its maiden flight on December 18, 1940, only to be wrecked in a major accident in February 1941. The US Navy had already placed an order for 370 SB2C-1s on November 29, 1940, but the first of these did not fly until June 30, 1942. The prototype was lost due to wing failure in December 1941 and the same fate was shared by the first production aircraft in January 1943.

The first of 7,140 Helldivers was delivered to the VS-9, US Navy in December 1942 but it was another 12 months before the type went into combat with VB-17, USS *Bunker Hill*, on November 11, 1943, against the Japanese-held port at Rabaul. The SBC-1, which replaced the Dauntless in service, was not popular with its crews and it was not until the arrival of the more powerful SB2C-4 (Model 84F) that the Helldiver's combat effectiveness began to improve, aided by improved handling. All but 26 of the 7,140 Helldivers built were pressed into US Navy service, such was the desperate need for dive-bombers in the Pacific theatre alone. The 26 were delivered to the Federal Aviation Administration as Helldiver Mk Is but were not employed operationally.

The Helldiver remained in US Navy front-line service until 1947 and the reserve until 1950. Large numbers of surplus aircraft saw extended service during the post-war period with many foreign air forces, including France, where the Aeronavale Helldivers saw extensive action in the First Indochina War until they were withdrawn in 1958. In the following year, the last Helldivers in service were retired by the Italian Air Force.

Production
In total, 7,140 SC2C Helldivers were built between 1940 and 1945. The main production variants were the SB2C-1 (200); SB2C-1C (778); SB2C-3 (1,112); SB2C-4 (2,045); SBF-1, -3 and -4E (300 built by Fairchild-Canada); SBW-1, -1B*, -3, -4E and -5 (834 built by Canadian Car & Foundry Co.) and A-25A Shrike (900).

---

* Of these, 26 SBW-1Bs for the Royal Navy were redesignated as Helldiver Mk I; type rejected and contract for 450 cancelled.

Technical data – SB2C-4 and SB2C-5 Helldiver	
ENGINE	One 1,900hp Wright R-2600-20 Cyclone
WINGSPAN	49ft 9in
LENGTH	36ft 8in
HEIGHT	13ft 2in
WING AREA	422sq/ft
EMPTY WEIGHT	(4) 10,457lb; (5) 10,580lb
GROSS WEIGHT	(4) 16,616lb; (5) 15,918lb (with extra fuel tanks)
MAX SPEED	(4) 295mph at 16,700ft; (260mph at 16,100ft)
SERVICE CEILING	(4) 29,100ft; (5) 26,400ft
RANGE	(4) 1,165 miles; (5) 1,805 miles at 150mph
ARMAMENT	Two wing-mounted 20mm cannons and two 0.30in machine guns in the rear cockpit, plus up to 2,000lbs of bombs in the fuselage bay and underwing racks

Right: Curtiss SB2C-4E Helldivers of VB-87 USS *Ticonderoga* in formation over the Pacific Ocean.

Below: The XSB2C-1 prototype, 1758, first flew on December 18, 1940, but was wrecked in January 1941.

SNC-1 Falcon (Model CW-22)

Development

Developed at the Curtiss-Wright factory in St Louis in 1940, the CW-22 was designed to be a basic military trainer and light-attack aircraft. A direct development of the CW-19B, which incorporated features of the CW-21, the CW-22 was another successful machine that sold in surprisingly high numbers.

Design

A low-wing all-metal monoplane, the CW-A22 housed two crew under a continuous glazed canopy. The main undercarriage retracted rearwards into the same type of underwing fairings that were installed in the original CW-21 but lacked the equivalent horsepower. The aircraft's main strength was its adaptability, and Curtiss marketed the aircraft as a sporting machine for the civilian market, or as a trainer, reconnaissance or general-purpose aircraft for the military market.

The first production aircraft was designated CW-22, followed by the improved CW-22B and finally by the CW-22N. The latter was ordered into service by the US Navy as the SNC-1 "Falcon."

Service

The prototype CW-A22, registered NX18067, first flew in 1940 and, not long after, a production order was received from the Dutch government for 36 CW-22s (serialled CF464 to VF-499) for service in the Dutch East Indies. The advancing Japanese saw the order delivered to Australia instead, in March 1942, where at least a dozen were attached to the 49th Pursuit Group. The CW-22s saw extensive action before they were reinforced by another order from the Dutch for 25 CW-22Bs. Several CW-22s were captured by the Japanese and operated by them. Fifty CW-22Bs were sold to Turkey and another 25 were spread between Bolivia, Peru and Uruguay.

One of 455 SNC-1 "Falcons" that were delivered to the US Navy during 1941 and 1942 pictured at Langley during evaluation on April 30, 1942.

After evaluating the prototype, the US Navy placed the first of three orders in 1940, designating the type as the SNC-1 Falcon. In total, 455 were delivered to the US Navy; the second and third batches featured a revised higher cockpit canopy. The Falcon remained in US Navy service until at least 1945 as a scout trainer.

Production

Approximately 592 aircraft were built, made up of one CW-A22 prototype; 36 CW-22s for the Netherlands; 100 CW-22Bs for export; and 455 SNC-1 Falcons for the US Navy.

Technical data – SNC-1 Falcon	
ENGINE	One 420/450hp Wright R-975-28 Whirlwind
WINGSPAN	35ft
LENGTH	27ft
HEIGHT	9ft 11in
WING AREA	173.7sq/ft
EMPTY WEIGHT	2,736lb
LOADED WEIGHT	3,788lb
MAX SPEED	198mph at sea level
SERVICE CEILING	21,800ft
MAX RANGE	780 miles
ARMAMENT	Two 0.30in machine guns, one fixed and one flexible

US Navy SNC-1 Falcon 6421 during a training sortie off the coast of Puerto Rico in 1943.

O-52 Owl (Model 85)

Development
A contemporary of the Westland Lysander and Henschel Hs126, the O-52 "Owl" was a two-seat reconnaissance and observation aircraft. A long time before the first aircraft flew, the USAAC ordered 203 Owls for a role that was still deemed necessary during the fragile peace of the late 1930s.

Design
The O-52 was a straightforward design. It was a high-wing cabin monoplane; its wings were braced with substantial single struts. The main undercarriage retracted neatly into the side of the fuselage, just behind the engine cowling, in line with the aircraft's profile although the wheels were exposed to the elements. Power was provided by a 600hp Wasp radial engine and the defensive armament consisted of a pair of 0.30in machine guns.

Service
The first production aircraft was 40-2688 (as there was no prototype) and it made its maiden flight in February 1941. Several were involved in USAAC military exercises after entering service a few months later, but it was clear that the aircraft's performance was not as good as hoped and the aircraft's reason for existing in the observation role was disappearing fast. In fact, following the attack on Pearl Harbor in December 1941 and the US's subsequent entry into World War Two, the "O" designation was scrapped in favour of "L" for Liaison.

Those that remained in service during the early part of the war were employed as courier aircraft and a few were employed on short-range anti-submarine duties off the US Atlantic coast, Gulf of Mexico and presumably off the Pacific Coast. Those Owls not employed in these tasks were relegated to training duties.

One of only a few surviving O-52 Owls, 40-2769 (N61241) was restored back to flight by the Yanks Air Museum in California.

The Soviet Union ordered 30 O-52s under the lend-lease scheme in November 1942. Only 26 were actually shipped and, following losses of ships on the Arctic convoys, just 19 were delivered. This figure dwindled even further when just ten O-52s were accepted into Soviet Air Force service. While the aircraft was not particularly popular with Soviet crews, this handful of machines were well employed in the task of artillery spotting, photographic reconnaissance and the Owl's original intended role of observation. Just one O-52 fell victim to the Luftwaffe while the remainder were kept airworthy, albeit in ever-decreasing numbers, until the 1950s.

It is not clear when the USAAF retired the O-52 but at least ten appeared on the post-war civil register under the Type "Limited" Certificate LTC-16 and by 1977 there were only three aircraft left.

Production

In total, 203 O-52s were ordered in 1939 with US Army serial numbers 40-2688–2890 at a cost of $50,826 each complete with military equipment.

Technical data – YP-60	
ENGINE	One 600hp Pratt & Whitney R-1340-51 Wasp
WINGSPAN	40ft 9in
LENGTH	26ft 4¾in
HEIGHT	9ft 11½in
WING AREA	210 sq/ft
EMPTY WEIGHT	4,231lb
LOADED WEIGHT	5,364lb
MAX SPEED	220mph
SERVICE CEILING	21,000ft
MAX RANGE	700 miles at half power
ARMAMENT	Two 0.30in machine guns, one fixed and one flexible

At least seven O-52 Owls are visible in the photo at Brooks Field in 1941. Many Owls were written off in landing and take-off accidents, including 40-2768 in the foreground, which was wrecked at Yturri Field after the pilot failed to lower the undercarriage on July 19, 1942.

P-40B and Tomahawk Mk IIA (Model H81-B)

Development
This stage of the long evolutionary road of the P-40 saw the aircraft brought into line with features that would become standard on all American-built fighters from late 1940 onwards.

Design
The P-40B featured a number of modifications that were applied across the industry in the US. These were self-sealing fuel tanks, extra armour around the cockpit, and a bullet-proof windscreen. In addition, the P-40B was fitted with an extra 0.30in machine gun in US aircraft, and for the RAF, a pair of 0.303in machine guns. While the P-40B was a more purposeful fighting machine than the P-40A, the additional weight that the modifications brought reduced the overall performance of the fighter.

Service
The first of 131 P-40Bs was delivered to the USAAC in January 1941 and with aircraft production now in full swing, the last aircraft was in service by April. The RAF received its first aircraft, designated the Tomahawk Mk IIA (Mk II was not used), from December 1940. The P-40B famously part-equipped the 15th and 18th PGs based at Bellows and Wheeler Field, respectively, during the attack on Pearl Harbor on December 7, 1941. While many P-40s were destroyed on the ground, a few managed to get airborne between the bombings to shoot down several enemy fighters and bombers. One of the P-40Bs at Pearl

An RAF Tomahawk Mk IIA in North Africa strikes an aggressive pose with its shark's teeth, a favourite choice of decoration throughout the P-40 family.

Harbor during the attack was 41-13297, which entered USAAC service in April 1941 and, later joined the 19th PS, 18th PG at Wheeler Field. The aircraft was undergoing maintenance in one of the hangars during the raid and survived undamaged, only to be wrecked later at Koolau Range, Ohau, on January 24, 1942. The aircraft remained there until 1987 when, in 2003, the wreckage was purchased by the Fighter Collection with the main restoration work being carried out by the Chino-based Aerofab.

In RAF service, the Tomahawk Mk IIA served with 2, 16, 26, 168, 170, 171, 231, 234, 239, 241, 268, 349, 400, 403, 414 and 613 Squadrons, and once withdrawn from operational use, saw extensive service with several OTUs in Britain and the Middle East. Like the Mk I before, the Mk IIA remained in service until late 1944.

Production

In total, 131 P-40Bs (Model H81-B) were delivered to the USAAC between January and April 1941, serialled 41-5205–5304 and 41-1329–7327. Another 110 Tomahawk Mk IIA (Model H81-A2) were delivered between December 1940 and September 1941 to Contract A-84.

Technical data – P-40B	
ENGINE	One 1,090hp Allison V-1710-33
WINGSPAN	37ft 3½in
LENGTH	31ft 8¾in
HEIGHT	10ft 8in
WING AREA	236sq/ft
EMPTY WEIGHT	5,622lb
GROSS WEIGHT	7,610lb
MAX SPEED	351mph at 15,000ft
SERVICE CEILING	30,000ft
RANGE	606 miles at 70 percent power
ARMAMENT	Two 0.50in and four 0.30in machine guns

One of the 110 Tomahawk Mk IIAs ordered by the RAF was AH973, pictured at the Buffalo factory before delivery. This particular machine was lost at sea en route to Britain; the only aircraft of the entire batch to be lost in such a manner.

P-40C and Tomahawk Mk IIB (Model H81-B)

Development

The arrival of the P-40C signified the end of the very first batch of P-40 orders made by the USAAC. Further modifications did nothing to improve the fighter's performance and many of the aircraft that survived the initial Japanese onslaught at Pearl Harbor and the Philippines were stripped down to remain in with a chance of dealing with the enemy.

Design

The P-40C was still powered by the same 1,090hp Allison V-1710-33 as its predecessors. The fighter featured a new fuel system with larger capacity self-sealing tanks. As well as the 134 gallons carried internally, the P-40C could also be fitted with a 52-gallon drop tank, which raised the aircraft's maximum range to 945 miles. The radio was upgraded from an SCR-283 to an SCR-247N, which was also retained in the aircraft supplied to the RAF. Standard armament was a pair of 0.50in Browning AN/M2 "light-barrel" synchronized machine guns and four 0.30in Brownings in the wings, while some of the RAF's Mk IIBs were reconfigured with six 0.303in machine-guns in the wings. All of the extra features of the P-40C saw the weight rise, the max speed reduce by a few more crucial mph and the ceiling drop to less than 30,000ft.

Service

The P-40C made its maiden flight on April 10, 1941, and by early June all had been delivered to the USAAC, although there is evidence that the RAF's Tomahawk Mk IIBs were already arriving in Britain from December 1940. The bulk of the P-40Cs were allocated to USAAC/USAAF stations overseas including the 15th and 18th PG at Wheeler Field, Hawaii, and the 20th PS, 24th PG based at Clark Field in the Philippines. During the attack on Pearl Harbor, approximately 60 P-40Cs were destroyed on the ground (only 25 P-40s were airworthy after the raid) and it was a similar story during the invasion of the Philippines, but those machines that did get off the ground and engage the enemy acquitted themselves well. It was a P-40C of the 33rd FS flown by 2nd Lt J D Shaffer, based at Reykjavik, Iceland, which scored the first victory of the USAAF on August 14, 1942, when he attacked an Fw200.

The Tomahawk Mk IIB was used extensively by the RAF and South African Air Force (SAAF) in North Africa and also with army co-operation units, flights and OTUs, just like its predecessors, until late 1944.

Production

In total, 193 P-40Cs were delivered between March and May 1941 with the US Army serials 41-1332843–13520. Another 930 Tomahawk Mk IIBs (Model H81-A2 and -A3) were delivered to Britain between December 1940 and February 1942 with RAF serials AH991–999, AK100–570, AM370–519 and AN218–485. Of these, 100 were diverted to China to serve with the American Volunteer Group (AVG), 26 (AN469 to AN485) were sent to Russia and lesser numbers were despatched to Egypt and Turkey.

Technical data – P-40C	
ENGINE	One 1,090hp Allison V-1710-33
WINGSPAN	37ft 3½in
LENGTH	31ft 8¾in
HEIGHT	10ft 8in
WING AREA	236sq/ft
EMPTY WEIGHT	5,812lb
GROSS WEIGHT	7,459lb
MAX WEIGHT	8,058lb
MAX SPEED	345mph at 15,000ft
SERVICE CEILING	29,500ft
RANGE	(normal) 730 miles; (maximum) 945 miles
ARMAMENT	(P-40C) Two 0.50in and four 0.30in machine guns; (Mk IIB) six 0.303in machine guns

Right: The RAF's longest serving Tomahawk Mk IIB was AK184, pictured in October 1942, which remained on strength with the Royal Aircraft Establishment (RAE) until December 31, 1944.

Below: Another 5 Squadron South African Air Force survivor was Mk IIB, AK431, which was transferred to 73 Operational Training Unit (OTU) at Abu Sueir.

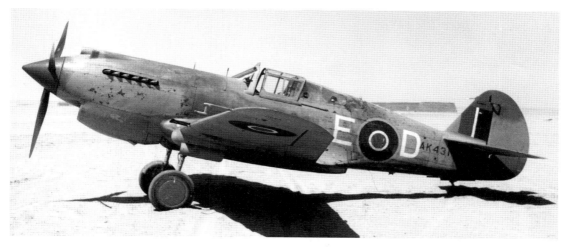

AT-9 Fledgling aka Jeep (Model CW-25)

Development

The USAAC began expanding rapidly in 1940, especially with regard to its twin engine medium bombers such as the North American B-25 Mitchel and the B-26 Marauder. The arrival of these aircraft created a need for a new type of twin-engined trainer, which was partly solved by the introduction of the Cessna AT-8. However, the USAAC needed a high-performance trainer that had handling characteristics much closer to that of a bomber, and this requirement was bridged by the Curtiss AT-9.

Design

The AT-9 was a low-wing cantilever monoplane with a fully retractable undercarriage, powered by a pair of 295hp Lycoming radial engines. The fuselage, which could accommodate a student pilot and instructor side-by-side, was a welded steel tube structure. The prototype was covered in fabric, pending an expected shortage of aluminium, while all production aircraft were covered in metal. A revised variant, the AT-9A, was installed with a R-680-13 engine and had revised hydraulics fitted for the undercarriage retraction system.

Service

First flown in 1941, the AT-9, was christened "Fledgling" by Curtiss, but in service was more familiarly known as the "Jeep." Deliberately designed to be less stable than the AT-8, the AT-9 was quite a difficult aircraft to fly and many pilots joked that the operational aircraft should have been used to train the pilot to fly the Curtiss twin-engine trainer first.

The Jeep entered service in 1942 but initially was little used because a large number of B-25s and B-26s were converted as trainers, which effectively took the intended role of the AT-9. The career of the AT-9 was short and many were placed in storage as more effective training aircraft were brought

Early production, quite possibly the first (41-5745) Curtiss AT-9 Jeep, described by many who flew it as a "hot ship."

into service. Because of the aircraft's challenging flying characteristics, the type was banned from the civilian market and was systemically scrapped.

Production

In total, 491 AT-9s were built, serialled 41-5745–894 (150) and 41-11931–12272 (341) at a unit cost of $44,965 and 300 AT-9As serialled 42-56853–57152 at $40,286 each.

Technical data – AT-9 and AT-9A	
ENGINE	(AT-9) Two 295hp Avco Lycoming R-680-9; (AT-9A) two R-680-13
WINGSPAN	40ft 4in
LENGTH	31ft 8in
HEIGHT	9ft 10in
WING AREA	233 sq/ft
EMPTY WEIGHT	4,600lb
MAX TAKE-OFF WEIGHT	6,000lb
MAX SPEED	197mph
CRUISING SPEED	175mph
SERVICE CEILING	19,000ft
RANGE	750 miles

A young flying instructor, who most likely is more nervous than the student pilot he is about send solo in an AT-9 at Randolph Field in February 1943.

P-40D/E and Kittyhawk Mk I/IA (Model H87-A/B)

Development

The next two P-40 variants introduced new model numbers and a new name, the Kittyhawk. It was this fighter that was to bear the brunt of fighter operations for the USAAF in the Far East and Pacific and with the Commonwealth forces in North Africa.

Design

The P-40D was the most extensively modified of the P-40 family to date, mainly because of the introduction of the Allison V-1710-39 engine. Originally intended for the XP-46, the USAAC wisely decided not to disrupt the production lines for a new aircraft and instead ordered Curtiss to fit the V-1710 into the P-40. The new engine had a spur gear reduction that pushed the thrust line 6in higher; this, combined with a larger repositioned radiator, gave the P-40D a different look from its predecessors. The cross section of the fuselage was slightly reduced, the undercarriage made shorter and 175lbs of armour were installed. Both fuselage guns were removed and a pair of 0.50in machine guns were placed in each wing, plus provision was made for a pair of 20mm cannons, which were never fitted. Shackles under the fuselage could handle a 51-gallon fuel tank or a single 500lb bomb and additional racks under the outer wings could hold six 20lb bombs.

The P-40E differed in having six 0.50in machine guns, three in each wing, which entailed the deletion of the unused cannon mounts. The Kittyhawk Mk I was the same as the P-40D, and the Mk IA was basically the export version of the P-40E, although they were delivered as P-40E-1s.

Service

The RAF ordered the Kittyhawk Mk I in May 1940 and it made its maiden flight on l May 22, 1941. It was identified by Curtiss as the Hawk 87-A2 and as the P-40D by the USAAC, which did not order the fighter until September 1940. The RAF order was delivered between September 1941 and April 1942 and the first 20 aircraft were installed with four 0.50in machine guns while the remainder of the 560-strong batch had six wing guns.

While only a handful of P-40Ds entered service, the P-40E served the USAAF extensively, especially with the 1st AVG in China where they were used very effectively against the Japanese. The P-40E also saw action from northern Australia and as the Kittyhawk Mk IA, the variant continued to keep the British and Commonwealth forces in contention in North Africa.

Production

Twenty three improved P-40Ds (Model H87-A2) were built, followed by 820 P-40Es (Model 87-B2). Another 560 Kittyhawk Mk Is (Model A87-A2 comparable to P-40B) and 1,500 Kittyhawk Mk IAs (Model H87-A3 and -A4 [designated P-40E-1 in US]) were built. Of the Mk I batch, 72 were diverted to Canada and 17 to Turkey. Of the Mk IA batch, 163 were allocated to the Royal Australian Air Force (RAAF), 12 to the Royal Canadian Air Force (RCAF) and 62 to the Royal New Zealand Air Force (RNZAF).

Technical data – P-40	
ENGINE	One 1,150hp Allison V-1710-39
WINGSPAN	37ft 3½in
LENGTH	31ft 8½in
HEIGHT	10ft 8in
WING AREA	236sq/ft
EMPTY WEIGHT	5,922lb
GROSS WEIGHT	8,515lb
MAX SPEED	334mph at 15,000ft
SERVICE CEILING	29,100ft
RANGE	716 miles
ARMAMENT	Six 0.50in machine guns

A Chinese soldier guards a line of P-40Es of the 23rd FG at Kunming in China. The unit encompassed a cadre from the 1st American Volunteer Group (AVG) and the shark's teeth decoration was carried over from the famous "Flying Tigers."

1st Lt A T House Jr of the 7th FS, 49th FG "Screamin' Demons" taxies his P-40E *Poopy II* at Schwimmer, Port Moresby, New Guinea.

XP-40F, YP-40F and P-40G Warhawk (Model 87-B3 and 81-AG)

Development

This stage of the history of the P-40 was the most significant by far because the dependable Allison was about to be replaced by the Rolls-Royce Merlin. It was the fitment of this engine in the later variants that kept the fighter in production for much longer than originally envisaged.

Design

In 1941, P-40D, 40-360, was modified to take a British-built, 1,300hp Rolls-Royce Merlin 28 with a single-stage, two-speed supercharger. The aircraft was redesignated as the XP-40F and subsequent P-40F production machines were fitted with an American-built Packard Merlin. 40-360, while a second aircraft, 41-13602, which was actually the third production P-40F, became the second prototype with the designation YP-40F. This aircraft had the coolant system repositioned further aft in several different positions including inside a thickened wing-root section. The aircraft was also used to trial modified tails and rudders with varying surface areas.

XP-40G was an unofficial designation applied to ex-P-40 39-221, after it was fitted with a set of Tomahawk Mk II (Model H81-A2) wings with four 0.30in machine guns. Forty-three P-40Gs were converted from P-40s between August and September 1941.

XP-40F, 40-360 (ex-P-40D) after it was fitted with the Rolls-Royce Merlin 28 engine; the distinguishing feature of the conversion is the lack of carburettor air scoop on the top of the upper forward fuselage

Service

The XP-40F Warhawk, 40-360, made its maiden flight with a Merlin engine installed on June 20, 1941, and remained a useful test vehicle until it was grounded at Lincoln on September 16, 1942. It is not clear when the second prototype, YP-40F 42-13602, made its maiden flight but as it was a production aircraft it would have been by late 1941. The aircraft was used for experimental flying until it was retired to Moore Field on October 8, 1943.

Sixteen P-40G were shipped to the USSR from October 1941, while the remainder served the USAAF in various capacities until October 1942 when they were all redesignated as the RP-40G. XP-40G, 39-221, was also shipped to the USSR in 1943.

Production

One XP-40F (40-360), was built, followed by one YP-40F, one XP-40G followed by 43 production P-40Gs. Sixteen P-40Gs were built and shipped to the USSR from October 1941.

Technical data – XP-40F, YP-40F and XP-40G	
ENGINE	One 1,150hp Allison V-1710-39
WINGSPAN	37ft 3½in
LENGTH	31ft 8½in
HEIGHT	10ft 8in
WING AREA	236sq/ft
EMPTY WEIGHT	5,922lb
GROSS WEIGHT	8,515lb
MAX SPEED	334mph at 15,000ft
SERVICE CEILING	29,100ft
RANGE	716 miles
ARMAMENT	Six 0.50in machine guns

The third production P-40F was used for experimental work as the YP-40F.

XP-60 series (Model 90/95)

Development

The P-40 was well-established by 1940 when Curtiss began to develop an improved version with superior performance. The USAAC was interested and that encouraged Curtiss to embark on a long and ultimately fruitless saga that would continue until late 1944.

Design

The design, which drew the USAAC in was basically a P-40 with a laminar flow wing, eight 0.5in machine guns and power provided by a Continental XIV-1430-1 inline inverted-Vee engine. A contract was awarded for two prototypes, designated the XP-53 (Model 88), on October 1, 1940, but before the design team could get into their stride, the USAAC cancelled the order, deciding it would like to evaluate the same aircraft with a Merlin 28 engine installed instead. The Merlin-powered aircraft was the XP-60 (Model 90) but a potential shortage of Packard-built Merlins saw the production aircraft installed with a turbo-charged Allison V-1750-75 and redesignated as the P-60A.

With the Allison engine, the P-60A would not meet the USAAF's performance criteria so Curtiss was instructed to build three more prototypes with three different engines. These were the XP-60A (Allison V-1710-75 with a GA turbocharger [Model 95]), the XP-60B (Allison V-1710-75 with a Wright turbocharger [Model 95B]) and the XP-60C (Chrysler XIV-2220 [Model 95C]). Curtiss recommended the Pratt & Whitney R-2800 Double Wasp with a set of contra-rotating propellers. A single four-blade propeller was fitted to the aircraft, designated as the XP-60E (Model 95D).

Service

The Merlin-powered XP-60 first flew on September 18, 1941, and on October 31, an order for 1,900 Allison-powered P-60As was placed by the USAAF. The aircraft's subsequent poor performance saw the order suspended, and on January 2, 1942, the request to build the XP-60A, B and C was made by the USAAF. The XP-60A made its maiden flight on November 1, 1942, followed by the XP-60C on January 27, 1943, by which time, interest in the project was already on the slide. The XP-60E (ex-XP-60B) was still not ready when the machine was requested by the USAAF for evaluation in April 1943 and, in its place, Curtiss quickly prepared the XP-60C for service trials at Patterson Field. The XP-60E was not evaluated until January 1944, but it was found to be a good aircraft compared to the P-47 and P-51. Curtiss was keen to abandon the project by then but USAAF made a final request for the R-2800-18-powered YP-60E, which first flew on July 13, 1944. Delivered to Wright Field, the YP-60E featured a bubble canopy but was destined to be flown only twice after Curtiss delivered the aircraft.

The development contract was cancelled in June 1943 but the whole exercise limped on until the last prototype was unceremoniously scrapped on December 22, 1944. The XP-60E lasted a little longer but was destroyed while trying to qualify for the 1947 National Air races.

Technical data – XP-60C	
ENGINE	One 2,000hp Pratt & Whitney R-2800-53
WINGSPAN	41ft 3¾in
LENGTH	33ft 11in
HEIGHT	12ft 4¼in
WING AREA	275sq/ft
EMPTY WEIGHT	8,698lb
LOADED WEIGHT	10,785lb
MAX SPEED	414mph at 20,350ft
SERVICE CEILING	37,900ft
MAX RANGE	315 miles
ARMAMENT	Four 0.50in machine guns

The last of the ill-fated XP-60 series was the 2,100hp Pratt & Whitney R-2800-18-powered YP-60E, 43-32763. While the first XP-60 first flew in September 1941, the YP-60E did not appear until July 1944.

P-40F and L/Kittyhawk II and IIA (Model 87B-3)

Development

Following the success of the trials involving P-40D, 40-360, with a Merlin rather than an Allison engine, the resulting production model was designated as the P-40F.

Design

When production of the P-40F Warhawk began, there was no block system in place, which categorized the aircraft made with each upgrade; this was not introduced until the 700th aircraft was built, which became the P-40F-5-CU. At this point, the fuselage was extended by 20in to improve directional stability. The block system identified the manufacturer that produced the aircraft and also highlighted the point in production when a modification was made. For example, the P-40F-10-CU introduced electrically operated cowl flap controls; the P-40F-15-CU was fitted with winterized equipment; and the P-40F-20-CU had an updated oxygen system. Power for the P-40F was the Packard Motor Car Company-built Merlin V-1650-1, which was rated at 1,300hp for take-off and 1,120hp at 18,500ft.

The P-40L was very similar to the P-40F-5-CU in many respects but was "stripped out," by lowering the fuel capacity to 31 gallons, reducing the armament to four 0.50in machine guns along with other equipment to lower the weight by 250lbs. Later P-40Ls were lightened again but this huge amount of effort to improve performance only saw a gain of 4mph over the P-40F at altitude. Follow-up modifications saw the P-40L-10-CU introduce electric aileron trim tabs and revised engine controls, the P-40L-15-CU had improved carburettor filters and the P-40L-20-CU had a new radio and various electrical modifications. Several P-40Ls were later installed with the 1,360hp Allison V-1710-81 and used as advanced trainers with the designation P-40R-2.

A USAAF Curtiss P-40F Warhawk beats up a field in North Africa in late 1942. Both the P-40F and P-40L served extensively in combat in the Mediterranean theatre.

Service
Deliveries of the P-40F to the USAAF began in late 1941, followed by the first Kittyhawks to the RAF from June 1942, although the RAAF received the type in the North African theatre much earlier. In RAF service, the P-40F was the Kittyhawk Mk II while the P-40L was the Mk IIA; it was the latter that were actually delivered first under the lend-lease scheme. Large numbers of RAF aircraft were diverted to USAAF and Armée de l'Air units operating in North Africa and the Mediterranean. The USAAF also transferred extra P-40Fs to the French including GC II/5, which flew the type in combat in Tunisia and along the Mediterranean coast until mid-1944.

Production
In total, 1,311 P-40Fs were built and 700 P-40Ls; 53 of the latter were later converted to P-40R-2 trainers in 1944. The RAF ordered 150 Kittyhawk Mk IIAs (P-40L [FL219-FL368]) and 100 Kittyhawk Mk IIs (P-40F [FS400-FS499]) with deliveries commencing from June 1942 and continuing until May 1943.

Technical data – P-40F	
ENGINE	One 1,240hp Packard Merlin V-1650-1
WINGSPAN	37ft 3½in
LENGTH	31ft 7²⁄₃₂in; (P-40F-5 onwards) 33ft 4in
HEIGHT	10ft 7¾in
WING AREA	236sq/ft
EMPTY WEIGHT	6,190lb
GROSS WEIGHT	8,674lb
MAX SPEED	370mph at 22,000ft
SERVICE CEILING	32,000ft
MAX RANGE	752 miles
ARMAMENT	Six 0.50in machine guns, one 500lb bomb

Curtiss P-40L-5-CU Warhawk, 42-10554, pictured during trials on January 29, 1943. The P-40L was one of many attempts to improve the performance of the P-40 family, and in this case featured a reduced weight.

P-40K and M/Kittyhawk III (Model 87)

Development

There was no doubting that the installation of the Merlin engine had improved the overall performance of the P-40 but the license-built engine was in short supply, and the USAAF had no choice but to bring the Allison engine (albeit a more powerful version) back on to the production line.

Design

The P-40K was installed with the much-improved Allison V-1710-73 engine, which was rated at 1,325hp during take-off and 1,150hp at 11,800ft. Very similar to the late production P-40E, the P-40K could also be fitted with an under-fuselage tank and/or carry bombs. Subtle improvements were introduced, including the P-40K-5-CU with additional rotary valve cooling and the winterized P-40K-15-CU. The P-40K-1 and K-5 retained the original, shorter fuselage but, because of the extra power of the Allison engine, a dorsal fin was added to help control the swing on take-off. The longer fuselage was introduced from the P-40K-10-CU onwards.

The P-40M was basically a P-40K-20-CU fitted with V-1710-18 engine rated at 1,200hp at take-off and 1,125hp at 17,300ft. The P-40M-1 had much stronger ailerons, the P-40M-5 had better carburettor filters and further improved ailerons and the P-40-M10 had a better undercarriage warning system and fuel system revisions. In RAF service, both marks were named as the Kittyhawk Mk III.

Service

The P-40K was first ordered into production on October 28, 1941; an order for 600 aircraft was placed to supply China under the lend-lease scheme. Curtiss thought that this would be the last variant of the P-40 to be built and was prepared to bring the P-60 into production. The failure of the P-60 saw the P-40K order increased to 1,300 aircraft on June 15, 1942, with the first production machine leaving the factory in August.

The bulk of the P-40Ks served the USAAF in the Far East and the Pacific theatres and with the Chinese Air Force. Large numbers of P-40K-1-CUs were delivered to Britain as the Kittyhawk Mk III; the first of these had arrived in the Middle East by late 1942. The type also saw service with the RAAF, RCAF and RNZAF and 25 were diverted to the Brazilian Air Force.

The P-40M was produced exclusively for lend-lease under a contract, which was first approved on August 24, 1942; the first aircraft was rolled out in November. The majority of P-40Ms were delivered to the RAF, RAAF and RNZAF, again as the Kittyhawk Mk III. The Mk III served mainly in the Far East, with the exception of No 5 Squadron (SAAF), which operated the type in the Mediterranean from January 1943 until September 1944.

Production

In total, 1,300 P-40Ks were built, with deliveries commencing to the USAAF in late 1941. Of these 352 P-40Ks were despatched to Britain as the Kittyhawk Mk III under the lend-lease scheme August 1942 and February 1943. A total of 600 P-40Ms were built, 364 of this number were sent to Britain as Kittyhawk Mk IIIs, which were delivered between June and August 1943, although 270 of them were diverted to the USSR.

Technical data – P-40K and M	
ENGINE	(K) One 1,150hp Allison V-1710-73 (F4R); (M) one 1,200hp V-1710-18
WINGSPAN	37ft 3½in
LENGTH	31ft 8½in
HEIGHT	10ft 8in
WING AREA	236sq/ft
EMPTY WEIGHT	6,400lb
GROSS WEIGHT	8,400lb
MAX SPEED	362mph at 15,000ft
SERVICE CEILING	32,000ft
MAX RANGE	350 miles with a 500lb
ARMAMENT	Six 0.50in machine guns, one 500lb bomb

Right: **Kittyhawk Mk III, FR243, of 250 Squadron, a unit that saw action through North Africa and up through Italy between 1941 and 1945. The unit operated the Mk III from October 1942 to January 1944. FR243 went missing near Lake Ampolini on September 9, 1943.**

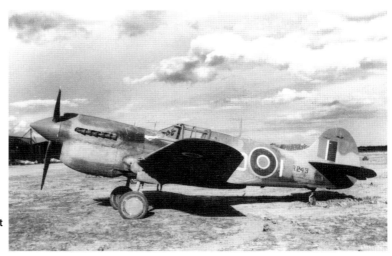

Below: **One of the more well-known RAF units, thanks to its use of the shark's teeth art, was 112 Squadron, which like 250 Squadron, fought its way through North Africa and on through Italy. This aircraft is Kittyhawk Mk III FR492; a survivor of combat operations, which was struck off charge on March 29, 1945.**

C-76 Caravan (Model CW-27)

Development
As early as 1941, a shortage of aluminium in the US threatened to disrupt production of the large number of all-aluminium aircraft already on order. While high-priority tactical aircraft such as fighters and bombers were generally protected, second line types such as trainers and transports were not. As a result the US government encouraged aircraft manufacturers to create aircraft designs that would use the absolute minimum amount of aluminium reserves.

Design
Curtiss-Wright's response to the requirement was the CW-27 Caravan, which the USAAF designated C-76. Designed by George A Page Jr, the CW-27 was a high-wing, twin-engine, cargo/transport aircraft with a tricycle undercarriage. The main cargo hold of the aircraft was low to the ground so that loads could be transferred to the standard bed of a lorry via a large upward hinged cargo door or conventional side doors. Loads as bulky as a Willies-type jeep or artillery gun could be carried. The cockpit was mounted on top of the aircraft so as not to disrupt the cargo hold.

Choosing not to copy the same balsa and ply used to build the de Havilland Mosquito, Curtiss took the advice of the Forest Products Laboratory and used the much heavier mahogany. Army Materials Command supplied the mahogany, and several furniture manufacturers were sub-contracted to build components for the CW-27, which would be assembled in the new factory at Louisville, Kentucky.

Service
Contracted to build 11 pre-production aircraft, the first of these, 43-86918, made its maiden flight from Louisville on May 3, 1943. It was an unnerving first flight with a number of serious vibrations occurring throughout the aircraft before the test pilot quickly set it down again. It was an ominous

The first of 11 YC-76 Caravan prototypes, 42-86918, built in the Louisville plant.

sign and, only one week later, the aircraft was lost when its tail unit broke away, killing test crew Ed Schubinger, John L Trowbridge and Robert G Scudder.

In the meantime, measures put in place to raise the rate of aluminium production quickly came into effect and the reality of aircraft made from wood soon lost its appeal. On August 3, 1940, after just 25 C-76 Caravans had been built, the whole project was cancelled. A large production order for 175 aircraft was also cancelled; the bulk of this order was to have been built by Higgins Aircraft in New Orleans, which was still under construction. The company was later recompensed with a large contract to build the C-46.

Production

Just 11 YC-76 prototypes were built followed by five production C-76s and nine YC-76As; 175 C-76As were ordered but later cancelled.

Technical data – C-76 Caravan	
ENGINE	Two Pratt & Whitney R-1830-92 Twin Wasp radials
WINGSPAN	108ft 2in
LENGTH	68ft 4in
HEIGHT	27ft 3in
WING AREA	1,560sq ft
EMPTY WEIGHT	18,300lb
GROSS WEIGHT	28,000lb
MAX SPEED	192mph at 7,300ft
CEILING	22,600ft
RANGE	750 miles
ACCOMMODATION	One or two crew and 23 passengers, or 8,000lbs of cargo

A production line of C-76 Caravan's in Louisville plant in 1943 in company with an AT-9A.

Curtiss-Wright XP-55 Ascender (CW-24)

Development

In 1940, the USAAC decided it was time to rethink fighter design and invited the industry to propose "unorthodox" designs. The only criteria were that the aircraft should feature low drag, excellent pilot visibility, and heavy firepower. Only three companies submitted ideas; Vultee, Northrop and Curtiss and all received contracts to develop their designs. The Curtiss design was the most daring of the three and accepted with a great deal of trepidation. The aircraft, designated CW-24, was dismissed at an early stage but, rather than abandon the project, Curtiss continued to develop the aircraft at its own expense.

Design

The CW-24 was a swept-wing pusher with canard elevators originally proposed to be powered by a 2,200hp Pratt & Whitney X-1800 engine. A tailless design, the swept rear-mounted wing incorporated the ailerons, trailing-edge flaps and, close to the wingtips, fins and rudders, which were positioned above and below the wing. The fuselage was oval shaped and of all-metal construction. The aircraft was the first Curtiss design to feature a tricycle undercarriage.

   To test the feasibility of the design, a light-weight mock-up, powered by a 275hp Menasco C-6S-5 engine, was quickly constructed of wood and fabric. Designated CW-24B, serialled 42-39347, the aircraft first flew from Muroc Dry Lake on December 2, 1941, where it successfully proved that the design worked well. It was while this aircraft was being flight-tested that the USAAF showed an interest

The second of the three XP-55s built was 42-78846, which first flew on January 9, 1944. Thanks to the flight restrictions placed upon it, this aircraft is the only example to survive today.

again and an order for three XP-55s was placed on July 10, 1942. Due to the unavailability of the X-1800 engine, these machines would be powered by an Allison V-1710.

Service

The first prototype, serialled 42-78845, first flew from Scott Field AAF in the hands of Curtiss test pilot J Harvey Gray on July 19, 1943. The problems associated with canard designs soon made themselves known and, on November 13, 1943, Gray was forced to abandon the machine in an inverted spin after falling out of control, for 16,000ft.

The second XP-55, 42-78846, first flew on January 9, 1944, and already significanly underway at the point of the earlier incident, was placed under flight restrictions, which included no stalls allowed below 20,000ft. The third aircraft, 42-78847, incorporated many modifications, including increased elevator travel and an increased wingspan of four feet and was the first of the three to be fitted with armament. First flown on April 25, 1944, the aircraft was handed to the USAAF for evaluation in September but its performance and general handling, especially at low speeds, was either inferior or no better than fighters already in service. 42-78847 was lost during a display at Wright Field on May 27, 1945, while 42-78846 is extant.

Technical data – XP-55	
ENGINE	One 1,275hp Allison V-1710-95
WINGSPAN	40ft 7in
LENGTH	29ft 7in
HEIGHT	10ft
WING AREA	235sq/ft
EMPTY WEIGHT	6,354lb
MAX TAKE-OFF WEIGHT	7,930lb
MAX SPEED	390mph at 19,300ft
SERVICE CEILING	34,600ft
RANGE	635 miles
ARMAMENT	Four 0.50in machine guns

The third, much-modified XP-55, 42-78847, with an increased span wing and modified elevators.

P-40N, Q and R and Kittyhawk IV (Model 87V and 87W)

Development

By mid-1943, despite the best efforts of the company to improve upon a fighter that had its roots in the mid-1930s, the P-40 was falling behind the new order (the P-38, P-47 and P-51) with regard to performance. The P-40N was the final serious attempt to catch up with its competitors and, despite the fact it still underperformed, more than 5,000 were built.

Design

The original plan was for this latest batch of production Warhawks to be powered by the Merlin and designated as the P-40P. Instead, with shortages continuing for the Merlin, the 1,200hp Allison V-1710-81 was installed and the fighter was redesignated the P-40N. The P-40N-1 had a lighter airframe, similar to the P-40E, K and M, four gun armament, no bomb racks under the wings, a lower fuel capacity, more armour around the pilot's head, manual undercarriage and flaps and a modified oxygen system. Combined with the V-1710-81, the P-40N was the fastest production P-40, capable of 378mph at 10,500ft.

The many production blocks that followed continued to fine tune the P-40N, all with varying armament, fuel capacity and ever-improving equipment including two reconnaissance variants. Underwing stores differed with one variant able to carry three drop tanks, providing the aircraft with a potential range of 3,100 miles at 198mph.

Two P-40Ks and one P-40N were converted into the XP-40Q (Model 87X) with a modified cooling system in the wing roots. One of the most impressive P-40s of all was the XP-40Q, which featured a bubble canopy (first trialled on an XP-40N), clipped wings and squared-off wingtips. At 20,500ft, the XP-40Q could reach 422mph, which was still slower than the P-51 at a similar height.

Service

The P-40N first appeared in March 1943 and the majority of the 5,220 built were destined to be supplied to the RAF, RAAF, RNZAF and the USSR (1,097 alone) under the lend-lease scheme. The bulk of the type's operational flying was carried out in the Far East and Pacific theatres, the type being particularly suited to fighter-bomber and bomber escort sorties. Very few entered operational service with the USAAF; the P-40N was relegated to the training role while the P-47 and P-51 had re-equipped virtually all of its fighter squadrons. Many were re-designated as the ZF-40N and a number were still in service with the USAF in 1948.

The RAF, RAAF and RNZAF operated the aircraft as the Kittyhawk Mk IV from November 1943 until the closing months of World War Two, although in Commonwealth service, the Spitfire and Mustang became the predominant types.

Production

In total, 5,220 P-40Ns were built; 586 of them were despatched to Britain between March 1943 and January 1944, under the lend-lease scheme as the Kittyhawk Mk IV, although the first 130 were diverted to the USSR. Of this tally, 468 served with the RAAF, 35 with the RCAF and 172 with the RNZAF.

Technical data – P-40N-1 and XP-40Q	
ENGINE	(N) One 1,200hp V-1710-81; (Q) one 1,425hp Allison V-1710-121
WINGSPAN	37ft 3½in
LENGTH	33ft 4in
HEIGHT	12ft 4in
WING AREA	236sq/ft
EMPTY WEIGHT	6,000lb
GROSS WEIGHT	7,740lb
MAX SPEED	(N) 350mph at 16,400ft; (Q) 422mph at 20,500ft
SERVICE CEILING	31,000ft
MAX RANGE	360 miles
ARMAMENT	Four 0.50in machine guns, one 500lb bomb and two 100lb bombs

A flight of 80 Squadron Royal Australian Air Force (RAAF) Kittyhawk Mk IVs (P-40N-20-CU) led by Wg Cdr Geoff Atherton in his personal aircraft, A29-629 Cleopatra III.

Curtiss XP-62 (Model 91)

Development

On April 29, 1941, the USAAC put out a tender for a heavily-armed, high-performance, single-engine fighter. Curtiss won the contract with its proposal, designated the XP-62, and on June 27, 1941, a single prototype, to be serialled 41-35873, was ordered, with a caveat of making its maiden flight within 15 months.

Design

The XP-62 was a cantilever low-wing monoplane with a retractable tailwheel undercarriage. The aircraft featured an air-conditioned pressurized cockpit, the first time such a feature had been designed into a US-built fighter from the outset. Power was provided by the huge 2,000hp Wright R-3350-17 engine, then under development for the Boeing B-29 Superfortress, which was the heaviest engine ever installed in a single-seat fighter. To harness the power of the R-3350, the unit drove contra-rotating co-axial three-blade propellers. Armament was initially proposed at eight 20mm cannons or 12 0.5in machine guns, all of which were mounted in the wings.

The specifications of the XP-62 were regularly reviewed during the design and development, which originally required that the aircraft be capable of 468mph at 20,000ft. On August 2, 1941, Curtiss submitted a revised maximum speed of 448mph if eight 20mm cannons were fitted, which also raised the weight by over 1,500lbs. A further review on January 1, 1942, saw the contract revised again with the armament reduced to just four cannons and no propeller de-icing equipment, thus reducing the all-up weight. On May 25, 1942, the USAAF placed an order for 100 P-62s, only to cancel it on July 27 when it was realised that this could disrupt urgently needed P-47s already being built by Curtiss at the time.

Service

Work continued on the sole XP-62, but problems with the pressure-cabin supercharger and various engine modifications delayed the first flight until July 23, 1943. Not long after, the requirement for a single-seat high-altitude interceptor had passed and the XP-62 was cancelled after a short amount of flight testing in September 1943. Placed into storage at Wright Field, Ohio, the aircraft was scrapped on September 26, 1945.

Technical data – XP-62	
ENGINE	One 2,300hp Wright R-3350-17
WINGSPAN	53ft 8in
LENGTH	39ft 6in
HEIGHT	16ft 3in
WING AREA	420sq/ft
EMPTY WEIGHT	11,773lb
MAX TAKE-OFF WEIGHT	16,651lb
MAX SPEED	448mph at 27,000ft
SERVICE CEILING	35,700ft
RANGE	1,500 miles
ARMAMENT	Four 20mm cannons

The XP-62 was the heaviest fighter ever developed by Curtiss, the first to feature a pressurized cockpit and was fitted with heaviest engine ever to a single-seat fighter.

Curtiss XF14C-2 (Model 94)

Development
Before the US entered World War Two, the navy was already on the hunt for a new, high-performance fighter to operate from its carriers. Curtiss was duly approached and, on June 30, 1941, an order for a pair of experimental fighters was made to be serialled 03183 and 03184. At the same time, the US Navy also awarded development contracts to Grumman for the XF6F-1 (later Hellcat) and the XF7F-1 (later Tigercat).

Design
The US Navy stipulated that the aircraft, designated XF14C-1, should be powered by the untested Lycoming H-2470 liquid-cooled engine*. Development of this engine did not go well and, in the end, only one aircraft was built with an air-cooled Wright XR-3350-16 Duplex-Cyclone radial engine and the fighter was designated as the XF14C-2. The Wright engine, with its 18 cylinders, drove a three-blade contra-rotating propeller.

Structurally, the XF14C-1 fell between the XP-60 and XP-62, complete with folding wings and an armament of four 20mm cannons.

Service
The sole XF14C-2, serialled 03183, was completed in September 1943 and presumably was in the air before the year was over. Delivery to the US Navy took place in July 1944, by which time, the service had already chosen its standard fighter aircraft in the shape of the Grumman F6F Hellcat and the Vought F4U Corsair.

Technical data – XF14C-2	
ENGINE	One 2,300hp Wright XR-3350-16
WINGSPAN	46ft
LENGTH	37ft 9in
HEIGHT	17ft
WING AREA	375sq/ft
EMPTY WEIGHT	10,531lb
MAX TAKE-OFF WEIGHT	14,950lb
MAX SPEED	418mph at 32,000ft
INITIAL CLIMB RATE	2,700ft/min
SERVICE CEILING	39,800ft
RANGE	1,530 miles
ARMAMENT	Four 20mm cannons

* The H-2470 was later installed in the Vultee XP-54 fighter.

Basically a lighter version of the XP-62, the sole XF14C-2, finished in a non-standard overall white colour scheme, was an adequate fighter but was subsequently overhauled by the F6F Hellcat and the F4U Corsair.

SC Seahawk (Model 97)

Development

In June 1942, the US Navy asked Curtiss to submit a proposal for an advanced scout aircraft. The convertible undercarriage arrangement was designed to give the aircraft the flexibility to operate from aircraft carriers, airfields or even catapulted from warships. Designed to replace the pre-war Seamew and Vought Kingfisher, Curtiss's latest design was called the SC "Seahawk". The Curtiss response to the US Navy request was submitted on August 1, 1942, but it was not until March 31, 1943, that an order for two XSC-1 prototypes was issued.

Design

The Seahawk was an all-metal, cantilever, low-wing monoplane with foldable wings; the outer sections having a considerable dihedral. The seaplane version had a large central float, part of which could be used as an auxiliary fuel tank, and strut-mounted wingtip stabilizer floats. The central float also had two compartments within it to carry extra bombs, but when used in this capacity it leaked.

The land plane version of the Seahawk was designated SC-2 (Model 97D), had a fixed undercarriage, was powered by R-1820-76 with a circular cowling and featured a clear-blow canopy rather than the segmented version used by the seaplane. The aircraft did not see a great deal of action because of its late entry to the conflict but a few Seahawks were involved in the bombardment of Borneo in June 1945.

Contracts were clinically cancelled when the war came to an end in the Pacific and those machines that were already in service had been retired by 1949.

Service

The first of three prototype XSC-1 Seahawks, 35298, made its maiden flight on February 16, 1944, from Columbus. A production order had already been placed by the US Navy in June 1943 and, as a result, the aircraft was in service by October 1944, initially with units on-board USS *Guam*. The US Navy primarily operated the Seahawk as a seaplane but each product was delivered to the US Navy as a landplane because a separate contract to convert them had been negotiated with Edo (Earl D Osborne Company), which would manufacture the floats.

Generally, the SC-1 was operated as a single-seat aircraft but it could also carry a stretcher case in the rear fuselage.

Production

A huge 500 production SC-1 Seahawks (35298–35797) were ordered by the US Navy in June 1943 followed by second order for 450 aircraft. The latter order was cancelled on V-J Day after 66 had been built (93302–93367). Another 450 SC-2 landplanes were ordered but only ten (119529–119538) had been completed by V-J Day when the contract was cancelled.

Technical data – SC-1 Seahawk	
ENGINE	(C-1) One 1,350hp Wright R-1820-62 Cyclone 9; (C-2) one Wright R-1820-76
WINGSPAN	41ft
LENGTH	36ft 4½in
HEIGHT	12ft 9in
WING AREA	280sq/ft
EMPTY WEIGHT	6,320lb
MAX TAKE-OFF WEIGHT	9,000lb
MAX SPEED	313mph at 28,600ft
SERVICE CEILING	37,300ft
RANGE	625 miles
ARMAMENT	Two 0.5in machine guns and two 325lb bombs

A conservative design, the Seahawk gave the US Navy good service during the latter stages of World War Two, but the service's preference for the helicopter shortened the type's post-war career.

XBTC-2 and XBT2C-1 (Model 96/98)

Development
Originally ordered under the complex designation XBTC-1 by the US Navy on December 31, 1943, the crucial part of the designation, which gave away the aircraft's intended role was "BT" an abbreviation of Bomber-Torpedo. This was a new class of aircraft for the US Navy and the Curtiss aircraft was ordered along with the prototype Douglas XBT2D, Martin XBTM and the Fleetwings XBTK.

Design
A low-wing monoplane, the original XBTC-1 (Model 96) was to be powered by a 2,200hp Wright R-3350 radial engine, but priority was given to the Pratt & Whitney R4360-powered XBTC-2 instead because of teething problems with the original choice. Only two XBTC-2s were built with different wings; the "Model A" was fitted with a standard wing with trailing edge flaps while the "Model B" had full-span Duplex flaps, a sweeping leading edge and a straight trailing edge. The 3,000hp engine either drove a 14ft 2in-diameter six-blade Curtiss Electric contra-rotating propeller or 13½ft six-blade Aeroproducts AD7562 contra-rotating propeller.

While the XBTC-2 was under construction, Curtiss was awarded a contract for ten XBT2C-1s on March 27, 1945. Very similar to the XBTC, the aircraft was powered by a smaller 2,500hp R-3350 with a single propeller and had room in the rear fuselage for a second crewman. The aircraft was also fitted with a search radar inside a pod under the starboard wing.

Service
The XBT2C was the first to fly in January 1946 while the two XBTC-2s did not make their maiden flights until July 1946. Delivered to the Naval Air Test Center at NAS Patuxent River, both prototypes were lost in separate accidents in February and August 1947. In the end, the US Navy chose the Douglas design, which evolved into the Skyraider and the Martin design, which became the less successful Mauler. The nine XBT2Cs built had all been scrapped before 1950.

Production
Two prototypes were built, both ordered by the US Navy on December 31, 1943: one XBTC-1 (Model 96) and one XBTC-2 (Model 98) with serials 31401 and 31402 respectively. Both were constructed as XBTC-2s. Ten XBTC-1s were ordered in March 1945, but only nine were built, with serials 50879–888.

Technical data – XBTC-2 and XBT2C-1	
ENGINE	(C-2) One 3,000hp Pratt & Whitney XR-4360-8A Wasp major; (C-1) one 2,500hp wright R-3350-24
WINGSPAN	(C-2) 50ft; (C-1) 47ft 7 1/8in
LENGTH	(C-2) 39ft; (C-1) 39ft 2in
HEIGHT	(C-2) 12ft 11in; (C-1) 12ft 1in
WING AREA	(C-2) 425sq/ft; (C-1) 416sq/ft
EMPTY WEIGHT	(C-2) 13,410lb; (C-1) 12,268lb
GROSS WEIGHT	(C-2) 19,830lb; (C-1) 19,022lb
MAX SPEED	(C-2) 347mph at sea level; (C-1) 297mph at sea level
INITIAL CLIMB	(C-2) 2,250ft/min; (C-1) 1,890ft/min
SERVICE CEILING	(C-2) 26,200ft; (C-1) 26,200ft
MAX RANGE	(C-2) 1,835 miles; (C-1) 1,310 miles
ARMAMENT	(C-2) Four 20mm cannons, 2,000lb bombs or one Mk 13 torpedo; (C-1) two 20mm cannons, eight 5in HVAR and one 2,000lb or two 500lb or four 250lb bombs

One of the nine XBT2C-1s built, pictured in 1946. The aircraft was a very capable machine, but it was still the last Curtiss design to be ordered by the US Navy.

XF15C-1 (Model 99)

Development
The US Navy understandably had a quite a few reservations about jet-powered aircraft operating from aircraft carriers at first. Early jet engines lacked the necessary acceleration, even with a catapult launch, so the US Navy decided on a cautious approach when it ordered a composite powered aircraft from Curtiss in April 1944.

Design
Designated XF15C-1, the aircraft was a conventional-looking single-seat fighter. An all-metal cantilever low-wing monoplane, the XF15C-1 had a retractable undercarriage, upward folding wings and four 20mm cannons. Power was provided by two engines; the first was a traditional Pratt & Whitney radial, which was mounted in the nose and drove a four-blade propeller, while the second was an Allis-Chalmers turbojet mounted within the centre section of the fuselage. The turbojet, which was actually a license-built de Havilland H1B-Goblin, was exhausted just behind the wing, rather than through a long tailpipe to the rear of aircraft.

Service
The first of three prototypes, 01213, made its maiden flight on February 27, 1945, in the hands of test pilot Lloyd Childs. The event was carried out on piston power alone as no turbojet was installed at this stage. Following installation of the turbojet, flight trials progressed, only to be halted when the prototype crashed on May 8, 1945, killing Childs.

Following the resumption of the flight test programme with the remaining two prototypes, the rear tail unit was redesigned to a "T" configuration, an innovation that was many years ahead of its time. Both aircraft continued to perform well; on piston power alone, the XF15C-1 could travel at 373mph at 25,300ft and, once the 2,700lb J36 turbojet kicked in, the speed rose to 469mph at the same altitude. Developmental problems delayed delivery of 01214 and 01215 to the US Navy until November 1946, by which time the project had been cancelled.

XF15C-1 01214 was later scrapped, but 01215 survives today in original condition at the Quonset Air Museum, Kingston, Rhode Island.

Production
Three XF15C-1 prototypes were ordered in April 1944 and built at Buffalo with the US Navy serials 01213–215.

Technical data – XF15C-1	
ENGINE	One 2,100hp Pratt & Whitney R-2800-34W and one 2,700lb Allis-Chalmers J36 turbojet
WINGSPAN	48ft
LENGTH	44ft
HEIGHT	15ft 3in
WING AREA	400sq/ft
EMPTY WEIGHT	12,649lb
LOADED WEIGHT	16,630lb
MAX SPEED (both engines)	469mph at 25,300ft
INITIAL CLIMB	5,020ft/min
SERVICE CEILING	41,800ft
MAX RANGE	1,385 miles
ARMAMENT	Four 20mm cannons

The second prototype XF15C-1, 01214, complete with its T-tail configuration; the aircraft was the first Curtiss design to feature a turbojet.

XP-87 Blackhawk (Model CW-29A)

Development

The competition to replace the excellent P-61 Black Widow was a hotly contested one between Curtiss-Wright, Douglas and Northrop, with North American in the wings, presenting the Twin Mustang as an interim. An all-weather jet fighter interceptor was the order of the day with Curtiss-Wright producing the big XP-87 Blackhawk, Douglas the XF-3D Skynight and Northrop the XP-89 Scorpion.

Design

The XP-87 was a large all-metal, mid-wing monoplane with a high-mounted tailplane and a tricycle undercarriage with twin wheels on each unit. The two crew members sat side-by-side under a large canopy, and power was provided by four 3,000lb Westinghouse XJ34-WE-7 turbojets, which were mounted in a pair of pods under each wing. The same pods also housed the main undercarriage units.

Armament was, at first, to consist of automatically-operated nose and tail turrets each fitted with two 0.50in machine-guns and rockets mounted internally. The nose turret was built by the Glenn L Martin Company of Baltimore and was mounted on a moveable platform, which gave a field of fire through 180 degrees (90 degrees to each side of the centre-line). However, this configuration was changed to four 20mm forward-firing cannons by the time the aircraft was completed.

Service

Built in Columbus, XP-87 No.1, 45-59600, was transported by road, over a very carefully surveyed route, which avoided bridges and overpasses because of the height of the tail, to the Army Test Centre at Muroc Dry Lake. First flown on March 5, 1948, by Lee Miller, the XP-87 was redesignated as XF-87

In a potential deal that would have secured many jobs for Curtiss-Wright and the company's future for a least a decade, there was a lot riding on the success ofthe XP-87 Blackhawk.

in June 1948. The aircraft was a good performer and everything looked good even though it was 12 percent slower than promised and suffered from buffet at high speed. As a result, an order was placed for 57 F-87A fighters and 30 RF-87A photographic reconnaissance variants on June 10, 1948.

Unfortunately, Northrops XP-89 (XF-89) showed more potential during extended flight testing as a fighter and the F-87 order was cancelled on October 10, 1948, effectively bringing Curtiss-Wright's aircraft production to a conclusion. All funds were transferred to Northrop leaving Curtiss-Wright with one working prototype and the second aircraft, XF-87A, 46-522, which was fitted with two 5,200lb General Electric J-47 engines. Work was halted immediately and the two Blackhawks were scrapped not long after.

Technical data – XP-87 Blackhawk	
ENGINE	Four 3,000lb Westinghouse XJ34-WE-7 turbojets
WINGSPAN	60ft
LENGTH	62ft 10in
HEIGHT	20ft
WING AREA	600sq ft
EMPTY WEIGHT	25,930lb
MAX TAKE-OFF	49,900lb
MAX SPEED	600mph at sea level
CEILING	41,000ft
RANGE	1,000 miles

The Blackhawk with its 60ft wingspan was very big for a fighter.

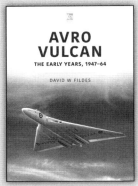

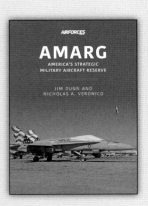